Singing to Donkeys

a life working for the Brooke Hospital for Animals

Lynne Nesbit

ISBN **9781514607022**

Cover design by dpdotcom with illustration by Ann Searight.

published by dpdotcom

To dear Andrew

With love

Lynne

November 2015

ACKNOWLEDGEMENTS

I wish to thank my publishers, dpdotcom, for their input, patience, generosity and support throughout the preparation and production of this book; Sarah Searight Lush (grand-daughter of Mrs Brooke) for her invaluable professional help and advice when editing my writings; Ann Searight for her drawing for the book cover design; current Brooke staff for their advice on content; the UK Trustees for all the help and support they gave me during my time at the Brooke, particularly Ann Searight, David Jones and the late Hilary Weir; all the many staff members, past and present, for their patience, goodwill, support and kindness towards a manager and co-worker on a perpetual learning curve (the chocolate cake on my 60th birthday was to die for!). There are so many who have played an important role in the story but I would particularly like to highlight with great gratitude the late Joan Hall, Richard and Julia Searight, John Trampleasure, Julie Carter, Suzanne Banks and Lesley Kirby. I also wish to thank my fellow legacy officers and managers in the many other charities with which The Brooke has shared legacies, for teaching me so much; Brooke trustees and staff overseas, past and present, for being the wonderful, welcoming, committed people they are; the amazingly generous supporters with whom I have had the privilege of being in contact, for their hospitality and goodwill towards me and for their abiding interest in The Brooke; and, last but not least, I wish to thank the countless animals, together with their owners and users, whom I have encountered over the years for teaching me humility, compassion, patience and gratitude. All of you, for me, make up the phenomenon known as The Brooke. For my experience of that phenomenon I am intensely grateful.

INTRODUCTION

Dear Reader,

In the time since my retirement, I have been mulling over the sweet wine that filled my thousands of days with the Brooke. My glass was never empty. It was often spiced with humour, warm with a hint of summer fruit. The rose was delicate, subtle and tinged with awakening possibilities. I thought it would be a pleasant occupation in my retirement to share a glass or two – or more - with whomever would be interested. There are many moments of delight, amusement, pathos, instruction and, without doubt, love. In fact, such moments cover the whole spectrum of human experience right here in our own charity. I love to write, so this is for me. Because it's for me, I shall allow myself to digress occasionally. When you are approaching 70, there is a lot to digress to, but I shall keep it to a minimum and only when I see a connection. But I digress….. Talking about the Brooke was always one of my most favourite occupations. Writing about it will help make more elastic the threads that will forever keep me within its ambit. It will ease me into the next life – retirement, that is, not the one thereafter…. And I hope it will make a bit of money for the animals.

Although I have many moments of equine connections to recall, there are a few Brooke office and other moments, too. "What a great learning curve!" is the usual euphemism for a certain amount of extreme discomfort! And you will laugh, as I learnt to. In fact, the conclusion I have reached so far – there can never really be a final conclusion in life – is that if I can laugh at myself in retrospect and gradually, carefully, on tiptoes and secretly, actually start to laugh at myself right now, life can be so much easier. Fun!

And writing the book is a way of saying THANK YOU!

Before we plunge in, for those who might not already know, I should just say a few words on what the Brooke Hospital for Animals is about. It is about a force of compassion, common sense and efficiency which is directed solely to alleviating the suffering of working equine animals – horses, donkeys, mules and ponies - which have to work unbelievably hard in extreme conditions in far-off places to earn a pittance for their owners or users. The combination of compassion, common sense and efficiency, when supported by generosity and intention, is indeed a force to be reckoned with. It can work miracles to transform the lives of the animals and the people to whom they are attached. In fact, although the Brooke is known generally as an animal charity, its work is so much broader than that definition implies. I would say that any charity's work is broader than its own definition. The subtle benefits ripple out so that everyone involved is touched by them in some way and the world becomes a better place. Everyone reading this will know exactly what I mean so I don't have to labour the point.

Returning to the charity I am actually writing about, the Brooke itself isn't about a quick fix to heal a wound. It is more about finding out what are the causes of the wound in the first place. So it works closely with its "clients" to see where they might be able to improve practices, improve husbandry. Theirs is not a "top-down" approach but a method which gives the power to the people, enabling them to look after their animals in a way which not only suits the animal but suits their owners, too. Often, the Brooke becomes part of the community it serves. It is there for the duration or at least until the lessons are learned and it can move on to other areas of need. I love to hear stories from the field where the people are taking it upon themselves to organise their own "best donkey" competitions, to install their own drinking troughs and provide the materials to build shelters for their animals. I love to see them perform puppet shows to teach their neighbours a better way.

In the period of the Brooke's history witnessed by me, and on which this book focuses (1982 to 2011) I saw a very small charity, whose work at the "coalface" was focused around three small clinics in Cairo, Luxor and Alexandria, expand into eleven countries worldwide and develop its methodology to become the leading charity in its field, a position it holds to this present day.

Mrs Dorothy Brooke founded the Old Warhorse Memorial Hospital in Cairo in 1934 (later to become The Brooke Hospital for Animals) in memory of the horses and mules so tragically abandoned by the British Army after the Great War. In her compassion, she had sought them out, bought them with the aid of donated funds and gave them a few days of loving peace before allowing them a dignified release from their painful bondage.

The importance of funding cannot be over-emphasised. Without the funds, nothing would have happened in those early years; neither could anything further be achieved in the years to come. The charity depends entirely on the generosity of its funders and has a close relationship with many of them today.

The Brooke continues to move forward. It is successful not only because it has a wellspring of intelligent and caring expertise within its teams both overseas and in the UK, but also because it isn't afraid to admit there might be a better way sometimes to carry out its work. It is continually developing its own practice. It will never stand still.

By the way, this little book is not meant to be a potted history of the Brooke Hospital for Animals; it is a random, non-sequential selection of cherries which I have chosen to pick from the orchard of my own memories. I hope you enjoy your reading them as much as I enjoyed my writing them.

So, here goes……

Chapter One

EARLY MOMENTS

It was a marvellous party! My current colleagues were all gathered together after work in the meeting room area. There were festoons of bunting and banners and a photo-montage. And so much delicious food….all provided by the guests. I could have invited so many people with whom I wanted to share my last moments as a Brooke employee, but space denied me that privilege. So if anyone out there feels left out, I am truly sorry. I did invite a handful of people from the early days, among them Richard Searight (Mrs Brooke's grandson and Organising Secretary), Joan Hall (who ran the London office for 19 years and who is now, very sadly, no longer with us but then was still gallivanting into her early 90s, bless her!), and Brian Thompson (our first Director, who is also no longer with us).   It was all great fun and I looked round the room at the shining, smiling faces – rather a lot of them – and couldn't quite understand how it had all happened. How had little Brooke Hospital for Animals come to be this expanding, vibrant, cutting-edge organisation, in the vanguard of its field, respected worldwide by organisations much greater in size, and making a difference to the lives of hundreds of thousands of needy animals and, probably, millions of people?

Some well-remembered Brooke moments, vignettes drawn from my own experience, might help to bridge the years of trial and error, success and failure, dogged determination, learning, skill, patience and, above all, sheer hard work by all concerned.

I am taken on!

It was early autumn 1982. I was walking up and down a street named Regency Street looking for the Brooke Hospital for Animals.   Alfred Marks Bureau had said this would be just the job for me – part-time, could take unpaid leave in the school holidays. Not too much responsibility. It sounded good. With two small boys, one of them about to go to Dulwich Preparatory School, I had to go out and earn his first school fees. £360 per term! And I liked the idea of donning a white coat and walking slowly between rows of quiet, well-behaved little things which needed a caring pat on the head. Perhaps I would carry a lamp…..

Regency Street is situated near the Tate Gallery. Not so easy for me on public transport from Greenwich. I could use the car, I suppose. But no-one knew of an animal hospital in the area. It was perilously near my interview time, so I rang the agency. "Oh dear, I'm so sorry, we put Regency Street by mistake. It should be Regent Street. If I were you, I'd ring them immediately." So I did. In a panic. A very kind-sounding lady reassured me that I could still come for interview. There weren't any others that day. I turned up - breathless and anxious, and very late.

But where were the animals? It was just a tiny office full of large furniture, with another office off to the right. The kind-sounding lady greeted me and made me a cup of tea. And a younger man with a benign face and a lot of hair (which he didn't seem to know what to do with as it fell this way and that) also stood up to greet me. Joan Hall and Richard Searight. Joan retired into the background (which was always her modest way), while Richard conducted the interview. I have the feeling that this was the first he had ever conducted; we covered all the necessary ground, Joan occasionally interspersing a timely remark or question and me offering unsolicited information which I thought my interviewer would want to know. But I was stymied by his last comment. "Well, thank you so much, Lynne. I will have to check with my aunt." His aunt? What did she have to do with the price of fish, as my mother-in-law would have said.

Well, it transpired that his Aunt was Pamela (Pinkie) Blenman Bull, Mrs Dorothy Brooke's only daughter. Mrs Brooke had had one daughter and two sons by her first marriage, one of whom, Major Philip Searight, was Richard's father and Chairman of Trustees. Pinkie still "ran" the charity from her home in Salisbury. Joan ran the office but kept Pinkie informed. The Trustees made all the decisions and Richard had also been brought in, initially on a part-time basis, because of his experience in advertising and public relations.

I was offered the job the next day and I accepted, mainly on the advice of Joan. "We think you are over-qualified for this position but would like to offer you the job anyway. And frankly, Lynne, with a young family, you don't want anything that taxes your brain too much. We shall give you school holidays without pay and you won't have to worry if the children are sick." I don't know about over-qualified....

What followed turned out to be eight of the best years of my professional life. Let me give you a taste of early Brooke office life.

True, I daily snagged my tights on the old wooden desk; there was hardly room to swing a…..stuffed teddy bear; and we might disagree on whether Beethoven or Mozart was tops for our choice of music while you work that day. And it was just a bit tedious to have to go to the ladies' loo to dampen the stamp sponge. But the compensations! For one thing, Joan and I were made for each other. We loved music - were both singers, solo and choral. Joan could identify every piece we listened to. We were both Friends of the Royal Academy of Art. We both loved cooking and exchanged recipes. We both loved Suffolk and shared cottage holiday nightmares.

We cried together at times, too. I remember two elderly sisters who would visit the office once a year. They wore their pale blue raincoats to match their blue-rinsed hair and had a little dog with them. Each year they presented Joan with a crumpled brown paper bag containing at least £300 in one pound notes which they had saved from their pensions and kept under the mattress. That was a lot of money in the early 1980s. We gently suggested that they save it in a bank account. Oh, no, dears! We don't believe in banks. We always had tears in our eyes when they left. One year, only one of them came – with the dog. Then, the next year she came without the dog. And the next year…..she never came at all. And we couldn't hold back the tears when we remarked on her absence.

A dog later played a key Brooke fundraising role. Sir Philip Shelbourne was a single gentleman who lived almost next door to Pinkie Blenman Bull in Cathedral Close, Salisbury. Perhaps it was this connection which had caused him to support the Brooke. He would also ring from time to time to order Brooke Christmas cards and have a chat with Joan. One year, he told Joan that his beloved dog had died. Joan replied that he would do best not to replace her immediately but wait. A dog would turn up. And, do you know, a dog did turn up! Just like that! It followed him into his office one day and never left him. I think he thought Joan was a witch, or something. Whether that had anything to do with it or not, being without immediate family, he left half his estate to the Brooke. By the time they had sold the house and its contents, our share notched up to over one million pounds! I represented the Brooke at his funeral, which was splendid and moving, in a fine City church. I also accompanied Ann Searight (one of Mrs Brooke's grand-daughters and a trustee of the Brooke at the time) to the preview of the sale of Sir Philip's chattels which had been mounted by Sotheby's in his home. Quite an experience! I almost dived for my National Trust membership card to cross the threshold!

Joan always chatted with supporters on the phone. One of them rang to find out a little more about us and requested a leaflet. Joan recognised the name Peter O'Sullevan as the famous racing commentator immediately and sent the leaflet first class that day. He returned the compliment with almost a gasp of admiration that she had acted so promptly. The relationship with Sir Peter grew, as he regularly bought our Christmas cards and then started to donate part of the proceeds of his annual charity auction. Although, very sadly, Sir Peter is no longer with us, his charitable trust is still as generous as ever and we remain ever grateful in return.

Dorothy Brooke's grave, Cairo

One day, I happened to take a call from a very agitated lady who had just returned from a holiday in Egypt. She wished to report a pregnant bitch which she had seen involved in an accident and could we do something about it. We were not really in the business of rescuing feral dogs and I explained this to the lady, saying that our funds were stretched to the limit looking after working equine animals, but I nonetheless took down the details of where she had seen the animal and told her that I would report it to our vets, assuring her that if they were in that vicinity, our vets would look for the dog. I duly did as I said. The vets recognised the area from the woman's description. Imagine my great surprise and wonder when I received a call from the Cairo Hospital: they had found the dog. It wasn't feral at all; it belonged to the man who looked after Mrs Brooke's grave! They treated the dog and told me it would recover from its wounds. I'm not sure whether it later gave birth. I reported all this back to the lady and I think she was mightily impressed.

Another phone call I received in those very early days, when I was truly lacking in expertise, came from a lady who wanted to know how to deal with her horses in her Will. What should she do with them? I had to think on my feet, intuition and common sense fortunately coming to my aid. I simply advised her to consider the short-term and the long-term needs of her horses, the short-term plan being of paramount importance. Both paths of action should be recorded in her Will but the short-term plan might have to be revised from time to time, depending on who was available. I advised her that she should consult whoever she wished to be involved before writing them into her Will. Surprisingly, some people don't think of that! With hindsight, I should have advised the lady to have her instructions in a signed Letter of Wishes lodged with her Will, since this would be easier to alter without incurring costs. That conversation proved to be a harbinger of many such with which I would deal in the future. It was also a real and memorable wake-up call for me; I managed to persuade my husband that we should write our Wills (he had thought it unnecessary) to ensure that we chose the guardians of our children ourselves.

The Fairs

There were always lots of visitors to the office, usually bringing us items to sell on our stalls at the Animals' Fair and the International Bazaar for Animal Welfare. How we managed to squirrel everything away, I shall never know. In suitcases, hat boxes, cardboard boxes and plastic bags. People brought all sorts of things, including one lady who always brought us simply a supply of paper bags. Nothing else, but that was so useful. I got to know her very well. She followed us to our next office and even though we didn't really need the bags then, I never told her. We had such amazing conversations. She had been closely associated with the Bloomsbury Group as an artist and writer; she always had something interesting, even profound, to say.

Another lady came each year with items which her employer had authorised her to select from the basement. One year, madam had told her maid to take something for Brooke's sale and she brought in a pair of neglected, rather forlorn and very dirty brass candlesticks. "I'm sorry, but this was all I could find." "Never you mind, we shall be able to sell them anyway, and thank you very much," said Joan. She cleaned them up a treat and they fetched £400 at Sotheby's!

Generally, we received gifts of the highest quality and saleability, though the used toilet seat and yellow plastic chandeliers were a bit of an exception. I reckon that the Brooke stall was always the best of the bunch. Even the clothes were excellent. Pricing, however, was an art. Not so high that they wouldn't attract custom, but not so low that it was insulting to the intrinsic value of the object and to the previous owner. We erred on the higher side as you could always lower the prices later. Packing and transporting the goods was also an art. There will be many readers well–versed in the anatomy of white elephants who will instantly recognise the understated attempt at sounding casual about this. There is no way round it. It was always *!?*+*£** hard work! We were blessed to have the services of our stationery supplier who generously drove me and the goods to the venues each year. It was his contribution. Once at the sales, you saw the highs and lows of human nature. There were those who would never even wait for their change and those who tried to bargain you down in pennies. One woman I got to know over the years had earned the reputation amongst stall-holders as a downright thief. She sometimes got away with it. We always had "look-outs" for such people but in the first onslaught of the opening rush, it wasn't always easy to see what was happening, especially to small items of jewellery.

One year, at the International Bazaar which was then held just off the Westminster Cathedral Piazza, we had some particularly good stuff for sale. There was an Egyptian musical box, beautifully worked with mother-of-pearl inlay, donated by none other than Major Searight. And there was a gorgeous hand-knitted sweater. I had put £25 on the box and £10 on the sweater. Well, you can only try…! When the doors opened, there was such a crush of people that they pressed the tables – and us – against the wall! I had stationed someone to watch the tables and kept the box playing, so that we could hear as well as see its presence. I was wearing a rather unusual cameo which my husband had given me – a head of Medusa set in pinchbeck. A man in the throng suddenly said, "Look at that brooch she's wearing! See what these charity workers get up to! They're in it for themselves!" I saw red! I must have turned the colour I saw. He would misread that, of course. Stupid of me to wear it, now I come to think of it. "Actually, it was a gift from my husband." "Ha! And I don't think!" So that unfortunate exchange set my inner landscape for the events to follow.

A little lady, perfectly spoken with her Chelsea accent and somewhat apologetic air, found her way through to the table. "Oh no, not her! Watch her like a hawk, please!" I recognised her as the one with the reputation. She picked up the sweater. "May I try it on?" Very apt words, I thought. "Well, no. You can buy it, try it in the Ladies and if it's not the right fit, we'll give you your money back." "Well, I'll leave you my purse which has more in it than the price of the sweater." "Okay, fair enough!" says I, somewhat reluctantly. Off she goes. Is that musical box still playing? Keep it going, keep it going. Little Miss Chelsea returns a few moments later. "I'm sorry but it doesn't fit." I sigh with relief.

So we carried on. Lots of sales, lots of pressure. The table was almost up against the wall and we were trapped behind it. "Oh, who sold the sweater? It's not here any more." Not me. Not me, either. No, said the third volunteer. I never saw anyone pick it up. Oh, yes, that little woman came back. She was looking at it again. Hmm! As the saying goes – shafted! I was furious, to say the least. More angry with myself for not noticing. And was the box still playing? Yes, thank goodness! Watch out for it. Listen out for it……

But, you know, we were so busy, our attention was taken time and time again, as it should be, by the crush of people wanting this and that. And, inevitably, we forgot to listen and look. Suddenly, I realised that our little song-piece wasn't accompanying us any longer. "Who sold the musical box? It's not here any more." Not me. Not me, either. No, said the third volunteer. The "look-out" said she saw a man pick it up and look at it. He was holding a white plastic bag. "Where is he? Can you see him now?" "There he is, on the other side of the room!" How I got out from the table trap, I'll never know. I scrambled underneath and came up like a deep-sea diver, red-faced and gasping for air. And I made a beeline for the man with the white plastic bag. He was in my sights but making for the exit. I battled my way through the throng. I had no idea what I would do if I caught up with him and certainly had no idea whether he actually had the box but I was so angry that I wasn't thinking of outcomes, just that very moment I was in. Intuitively, I knew the answer to the unasked question. And, as if to verify my thoughts, he speeded up; so did I.

Eventually, as the way became clearer, he got wind of me following him and broke into a run. Like a madwoman, I ran after him out onto the Piazza. He was large and middle-aged. I was small and middle-aged. But I felt larger than him. I had right on my side! I was on a mission! And, after the cameo brooch and the sweater, I was already very angry. I caught up with him and pulled at his arm, saying at the same time "Excuse me, but could you show me what you have in that bag." Naturally, he declined, somewhat less politely than I had asked. But I persisted as we moved across the Piazza together and even said "I have reason to believe that you have taken some things from our stall and want to check, please." To my astonishment, he suddenly stopped and said, "Oh, here you are – take the ****bag!" I did. The man hurried off. The bag didn't contain the sweater. No, that had become the booty of you-know-who. But it did contain the mother-of-pearl inlaid box and a few other things from our stall, as well as a collection of some unrecognisable stuff from other stalls. He had been quite busy. I stood there, shaking. I had just performed my first citizen's arrest. (Actually, I haven't repeated this feat since, so I hope it's my last.) I tried to find the right stalls for the other stuff in the bag. Not easy. So some of it ended up on our stall. And the box? We lowered the price to £20 and it sold immediately!

Chelsea Town Hall was another venue for animal charities to sell donated goods. As well as all the usual dealers looking for a deal, the crowd included tenants from the nearby Peabody Housing Trust, looking for a bargain. Neither were interested in good causes, just good prices. One lady found a pair of shoes which fitted perfectly. The only problem was that she had in her purse only enough money for her bus fare home and a bit over. Would I let her have them for the bit over? Well, they were good shoes. I remembered the lady who had donated them. I couldn't let them go for such a paltry sum. Yet this lady was also in need. It was near the end of the day. I might not get another purchaser anyway. I looked at her straight in the eyes and said, "You can take them home with you and send me the money." "Really?" "Yes, I trust you. I know you will." And she did.

Lynne emptying rainwater at the Arab Horse Show

The Arab Horse Show was an annual event which took place in two counties – Essex and Worcestershire. Our intrepid supporter, Dolly Langton, attended both with her trusty caravan and set up a Brooke stall. She had inherited it from a previous supporter who also set up shop at the Shows. This lady was also a judge, so Joan Hall and then I went along to man the stall. I continued to help Dolly whenever I could. It was all great fun, despite adverse weather, and Dolly made valuable connections for the Brooke. She also amassed an amazing amount of "valuables", some of them turning out to be valuable, to her surprise and pleasure.

Tea at the Commons

One of the highlights of the Brooke year became the tea-party at the House of Commons. We had wanted to celebrate our 50th anniversary and I said we should have a party for supporters, but where? Joan Hall suggested the House of Commons. She knew her local MP quite well and he arranged the permission. There were lots of hoops to circumnavigate but Richard and Joan managed to bring everything together. It was a huge success! Tea in the Members' Dining Room at the House of Commons! So many people came; there was a queue all the way along the magnificent pillared corridor leading to the rooms. And it was a splendid tea. We showed Richard's new video, we had speeches and we met so many faces belonging to the names we knew so well. Everyone wanted to come again the following year, and it became a tradition which lasted many years. Sometimes it was held at the House of Lords but the Commons had the vote for the most atmospheric venue.

We were not allowed to hold any kind of fundraising event, no auction or collection. However, one of our more enterprising supporters wasn't going to accept this. What was the point of gathering everyone together if we didn't ask them for money? But the Brooke was quite reticent about asking for money. People just sent it. We never had to ask. Our valiant supporter just decided to flout the rules of the House and took off her stylish hat! It was soon overflowing with notes which we stuffed away with great haste and embarrassment. And, I have to admit, not a little glee.....

Lynne sees it for herself

Richard Searight and his father went out to Egypt every six months to monitor progress. Richard is a very talented photographer and would return with some amazing photos, sometimes taken from the roof of the clinic or the top of a wall, to get that perfect angle. I saw pictures of our vets at work, of pitiful donkeys, for instance, working in the brick kilns which were visited regularly by our staff. The brick kilns cover vast areas around the outskirts of Cairo, providing the bricks to feed the ever-growing city. People live in buildings which appear to be unfinished. No top storey. The story goes that they will be built up later, when the next generation needs to house their family. Visiting the kilns is like visiting another planet, another world. The tall chimneys spike the sky and belch out their pollutants. Beneath them toil the poorest people and their even poorer animals, forming the wet bricks by hand and carrying them between the different stages of manufacture. Life is very hard indeed for a brick kiln worker and his animal.

Richard Searight directing major movie

And I saw photos of magnificent horses pulling the gharries – the tourist "traps"- in Luxor. Some were not so magnificent. Vying for trade and hoping to cram in as many customers as possible, drivers would whip their horses into frenzied gallops, while overloading their carriages with tourists. Our message around the town was always to choose only a well-kept horse and gharry and to stop your driver if he whipped his horse.

I was horrified by Richard's photos of the living conditions of the rubbish-collecting communities known as the Zabbaleen. In the days when the British Army was stationed in Cairo, the Copts ("Copt" means "Christian" and Copts are some of the earliest) would keep pigs to provide the men with their bacon. Muslims do not have anything to do with pigs. The Copts were (and still are) often the poorer, less-advantaged members of Egyptian society. To feed their pigs, the Copts would collect the rubbish dumped by Cairo's inhabitants and allow their pigs to scavenge for food. Eventually, they became the "official" rubbish collectors of Cairo and now collect from everywhere, be it domestic, commercial and even medical.

Richard liked to photograph the Cairo Hospital ambulance with our name emblazoned on its side. The ambulance had been purchased for us and fitted out to our specification by one Bob Brastock, who was renowned then as supplier of horse boxes to the Royal Family. I am sure that it is Bob's words of praise for our work in certain royal ears which would have initially aroused their abiding interest. Bob was such a character. And he kept a parrot. I once invited him to have lunch with me, but he said he couldn't, as he was having a sandwich at the Palace. How can one compete…? It was always a trial transporting an ambulance to Cairo. The vehicle would invariably be "detained" at Egyptian Customs and we would finally take possession, only to find it had been stripped of virtually its entire innards. Screws had been replaced with Sellotape to hold bits together. After this happened, we always had someone "camping" in subsequent vehicles until the notorious detention period was over. Now, of course, all our vehicles are sourced and fitted out locally.

I had been working for the Brooke for over six years before I finally had the opportunity to see the work for myself. Although the offer had been made earlier, I couldn't leave my children; I wanted to share this experience with my husband. We were still only operating in Egypt at the time. We had, however, opened the clinic at Aswan. The cheapest way to get to Egypt was on a package deal.

Anyone who has visited our flagship Hospital in Cairo will know what I mean by a right royal welcome! Well, here was Lynne coming from the hallowed London Office. I represented the founding mothers and fathers. Richard and his father paid their bi-annual visit and I know they were treated graciously but I didn't expect it to be quite like this. I really did feel like the Queen of Sheba. I think that even my husband was impressed – and that's saying something! But first we had to find the hospital. It was in a very poor quarter next to an abattoir. I wasn't too confident about our chauffeur. But the hotel staff had written the address in Arabic and explained the location to our driver, so we just had to trust. After what seemed like a very long time driving along main roads, over bridges and flyovers, and then threading our way through narrow streets, full of people and donkeys and carrots and tyres and bread and overhead wires and unfinished buildings, we finally arrived. And there it was, just like the photos! Painted a soft reddish American barn colour with the large familiar sign – The Brooke Hospital for Animals.

We opened the swing doors and entered. It was so quiet and peaceful in contrast with the cacophony outside, that I thought I should hear an organ play any minute. It truly had the atmosphere of a church. Tiptoe-ingly quiet. A bucket clanged somewhere, like a bell calling us to prayer. And Brigadier Hassan Sami the Director, and Youssef the Accountant, and Drs Salah, Nagi and Amira the vets, were all lined up to greet us. And Mustapha, one of the drivers. He had already been there a hundred years. Here's a digression: once, Mustapha was driving Brigadier Sami and myself somewhere and calmly drove up a one-way street the wrong way. I looked at Sami with some consternation and pointed to the arrow. Sami smiled and said, "It's okay. He does it all the time." It seems that no-one places much importance on road signage in Cairo. One of the most endearing qualities of Egyptians is their ability to laugh at themselves, gently. I must learn the art…..

Brigadier Hassan Sami was known to the Brooke in England as Sami. No-one else in Egypt ever called him that! He was either Brigadier Sami or Hassan, if you knew him better. But to us he was always known as Sami and he didn't seem to mind. Sami was the nephew by marriage of Dr Murad.

Ah… Dr. Murad. Let me tell you now about Dr Murad Raghib, the most dedicated of vets, who had been with Mrs Brooke from the start and whom I had the privilege to meet when he came to London some years before to receive his OBE. Dr Murad lived in a little flat above the hospital so that he was always on call. He had been devoted to Dorothy Brooke and was singularly devoted to her Hospital after she died. For some reason, every female supporter who came within three feet of him fell in love with the man. Perhaps devoted Dr Murad needed some help warding off all these unwanted would-be devotees. But Dr Murad was totally committed to the animals and he was undiverted. His voice and touch were the gentlest of gentle. But, though saintly in his attitude to animals, he was a tyrant about his veterinary methods. Nothing could be done that differed from them in the slightest. He had the highest standards for his time.

Dr Murad Raghib with Richard Searight

Brigadier Sami had been appointed to help Dr Murad with the administrative side of things only two weeks before my own appointment. He had been an officer in the Egyptian Army and had a degree in psychology (which I think he employed incessantly!). He and I got to know each other very well over the years and there is a great deal of mutual respect between us. He is an acute observer of human nature and a negotiator par excellence, which would come in very handy when it came to dealing with the police, as well as with self-important local potentates who might want to stop us from installing a water trough or give us land to build a clinic - but with strings attached. The police gave us permission to visit the rubbish collecting areas which were generally not places frequented by the public. They also helped us if owners were flagrantly flouting the law, particularly in the rougher markets. Troughs are vital to the horses and donkeys but not so popular with local residents. Permission had to be sought from the local town mayor. Even when granted, only a few years might pass before the trough is summarily removed for no good reason. And land might be offered on which to build a clinic which turns out to be a much desired memorial in the dreams of a retiring local official. Brigadier Sami was expert in ascertaining the hidden conditions behind such apparently generous offers.

Open space at Cairo Hospital

By the time I visited Cairo myself for the first time, Murad had passed away and Sami was in sole charge, with his vets and their fleet of teams reporting to him. At that time, the staff was still small. Drs. Salah and Nagi had assistants to help them with their outreach work. Dr Amira was our lady vet then responsible for the small animals' clinic. In those days, people would bring their dogs and cats, sheep and goats, as well as equids. If they could afford to pay, we asked for a fee. Otherwise treatment was free and the vets would never turn any animal away. I remember, during one visit when travelling to the Luxor clinic in a bus with supporters, we stopped to pick up a lady with a budgerigar in a cage. She wanted a lift to the clinic, seeking treatment for her budgie! Eventually, we stopped the small animals' service as it was detracting the Hospital's attention from its main purpose. But, even now, the Hospital never turns away an animal in need.

Rubbish, Mokattam Hills

After coffee and a chat, David (my husband) and I were taken on our first tour of the Hospital. I was not a horsey person at all. I had been thrown off a horse at the age of twelve and never got back on again. (This was a far cry from the person who spent time the day before writing this communing with a wonderful, intelligent mare who breathed into my face and brushed my cheek with her nose. I noted the change in my "horseyness" as I walked away from such a moving encounter.) So I, the yet-to-be horse lover, watched cautiously from a distance as we were introduced to each inmate and had its wounds or illness explained to us. Everything was slow, gentle and quiet, as though time had virtually stopped. We were taken to the isolation ward. That was when I cried for the first time. There was something so pathetic and vulnerable about the inmates there.

Children collecting rubbish, Maadi (vicinity of Hospital)

Then it was time to be taken to the Mokattam Hills with Dr Nagi, and we travelled with him in the mobile clinic. Fortunately, Dr Nagi could speak a modicum of English. The Mokattam Hills is an area where some of Cairo's rubbish collecting community live. It was a huge area, a shanty town on steep slopes comprising buildings made from refuse, some made with bricks and others of corrugated iron. Imagine that in the heat of summer. There was a pall of smoke over the place. The air was carbonated. Rubbish was burning in piles here and there. Everywhere. At the time of my visit, there was a road going into the place, thanks to Brooke, which had used all its influence to make sure it was built. Before the road was built, donkeys pulled carts through the burning rubbish to their owners' dwellings. Up to their fetlocks in the stuff. We had to treat many burns then, of course.

Our mobile clinic stopped and people started to gather. Dr Nagi spoke enough English to explain what was going on. Although burns were still usually high on the list, that day he was mostly treating donkeys with sores and eye infections. One boy brought up his donkey, limping. The poor creature had a nail in his foot.

At least the boy had noticed this fact. Dr Nagi wanted to bring the donkey into the clinic to treat the foot and make sure it stayed clean for a few days. The boy went to ask his father but the man refused to have his donkey taken away from him. So Dr Nagi told him it would be the man's responsibility to keep the wound clean for the next couple of days until the Brooke's next visit. Did he have any clean, sterile cloth? What a question, I thought! Here? Why didn't Dr Nagi provide it? But the man returned with some spotlessly white linen and he promised to keep the wound clean himself. I came to understand that we didn't spoon-feed people. Later, I saw the local barber working with his clients outside, again each tied with a spotlessly clean piece of linen round his neck. We passed a group of strange, round, brick-built mounds. These were the community's bread ovens. As Dr Nagi worked, I tried to make conversation with the people, who were gathering to look at David and me with great interest. I spotted two red-headed boys and made a beeline for them. My own boys have red hair. I told their mother that, with the help of elaborate gestures, and lovingly patted them both on the head. Shouldn't have done that...... Crawling with lice.......

We moved on past the many machines noisily grinding away plastic which would be sold for recycling, past the piles of cardboard, piles of corrugated iron and other rubbish which was waiting to be sorted by hand, I was told, after I had been shaking everyone's hand! Please, dear God, remind me to wash my hands at the earliest opportunity. Each family had their own pile which was added to daily by the children, after dawn expeditions on their donkey carts. If they were lucky, there might be a school run by nuns nearby, to which they would go afterwards. If they were even luckier, father would have a motorised vehicle to collect the rubbish, but there weren't many of those. A woman beckoned to me to come into her "house". It had a brick-built front but the rest was made of corrugated iron. Dr Nagi signalled that it was okay. Apparently, she wanted to show me her new piglets. I went through the low doorway into the one room which appeared to serve all purposes. But I wasn't prepared to come face-to-face with a large four-poster bed covered with a beautiful patchwork quilt! Where was I? And on the other side of the room was her prized large black pig with several equally black and very silky piglets suckling away. They were beautiful! At the back of the room was an exit leading to an area occupied by a huge mound of rubbish waiting to be sorted…..by hand….

Mustapha, Brigadier Hassan Sami and Dr Amira

We shook hands, of course, and I admired her piglets. Frankly, I was even more interested in the quilt! This was an unforgettable moment in my life. The lady's welcome was warm, dignified and totally open. She wanted to share her delight in the piglets and I was deeply touched. Suddenly the world was smaller in size. Humanity is one enormous family, in truth. I felt connected to this lady in a way that I would not have imagined before.

We returned for a very late lunch at the hospital. Yes, I did remember! In fact, lunch was served in the little flat which used to house Dr Murad. Strangely, Sami didn't join us, though he served us. (I later learned that this was normal custom with guests.) The meal had been cooked by Mustapha, the chauffeur. He had especially gone to the butcher to buy the best meat and also the best bread. There was a selection of vegetables, pulses, rice and other dishes. The table was groaning. But David and I were the only ones sitting at it! And we had totally forgotten to mention that we didn't eat meat. Of course, there was only one thing to do in those circumstances – eat it! I looked at David; David looked at me. Okay, in for a penny……. The meat was served on skewers and I picked one up and took a bite. It was rather chewy. In fact, I chewed away for some time without making any inroads. I don't know what animal it had come from but he must have had a long and stressful life! Or he was fresh as a daisy - hadn't been hung long enough. Was it camel, or goat, or horse?

After some time, I looked at David in consternation. He was having the same difficulty. In the end, we had to time our chewing so that, when Sami's back was turned, we could transfer the poor animal's remains from mouth to pocket. I don't know how I survived that meal. I felt embarrassed and awkward to the hilt. And Mustapha had really pulled out all the stops to create the very best feast for his important guests. We did our best with the rest of the dishes but had to admit defeat eventually. We returned to our hotel to rest, digest and be ready for the next day's visit – to a donkey market. I recall it was the notorious Imbaba Market.

This was a different kettle of fish entirely. What was I saying about the Family of Mankind? Hmm…. We were told not to stray too far from the vehicle and that I should not be left alone at any time. There were groups of men talking and haggling over donkeys in various states of health. One was pretty poor and the vet went over to it immediately. The problem can then be establishing whom to speak to about the animal. If it has been newly bought, the new owner naturally doesn't want to take responsibility for its state of health, which had occurred before he took the animal, and the former owner also doesn't want to take responsibility. That's one reason why the price is so low, isn't it? Faces and attitudes are hard in the market. The animals are beaten mercilessly and we have actually filmed one owner in the common practice of forcing a horse to pull a cart with locked wheels, to demonstrate its strength. (You might have seen this in our famous television programme "Cairo Vets" which was aired by the BBC in 1989.) Although this practice has been outlawed, it still takes place. The police look on. One of our vets was actually knifed by an owner for remonstrating with him over this practice. I was pleased to leave such a place. The Chelsea Animals' Fair and the International Bazaar for Animal Welfare were a doddle after this…..!

The next day we were off duty to do some sightseeing in Cairo before leaving in the evening for Luxor. We were taking the night train.

If you want to go to Luxor the slow way, with time to enjoy your own company and wake up in the morning to a biblical view of water wheels, buffalo and sunrise over the canal, the experience of being on a train in Egypt is for you. Ours never went above 30 miles per hour.

Apparently, this was because the train ahead was going at 30 m.p.h. But it gave us time to work out our sleeping arrangements on narrow bunks, sharing with strangers in the same carriage, enjoying a delicious breakfast of breads and jam and coffee and looking at those villages sliding slowly by along the banks. This was rural Egypt, so different from the polluted atmosphere of Cairo. Time seemed to have stood still, frozen in an age belonging to the Bible's patriarchs. As we moved further south, the buildings no longer had roofs but simple thatch laid across mud brick walls. Women carried water pots on their heads with graceful ease. Flocks of snowy white egrets were blossoming on the trees like masses of cotton wool tufts.

The Luxor clinic was beautiful. Small. Picturesque. Its wrought iron gates opened onto a little courtyard, in the middle of which was a large, shady tree. The stalls were ranged in a circle around, with offices and little storage rooms. People came and went. We watched a horse being shod by the clinic's farrier. Again, there was an atmosphere of tranquillity and rest. Just what the occupants needed. In those days, most of the work came to the clinic, rather than the clinic seeking out the work. There were both donkeys and horses, although, being a tourist city, carriage horses abound and have always been some of our main clients in Luxor City.

Now, however, at the time of writing, the situation is different. We have been established in Luxor for a very long time and the carriage horse owners have, in the main, got the message, though there will always be some rogues. The Luxor clinic's original location was on the site of ancient monuments, very close to the Luxor Temple. For years we had been threatened with closure to make way for excavations. It finally came to pass a few years ago and we are currently located outside the city. Now, we mainly go to the work, rather than it coming to us, as before. Our veterinary ambulances go to a variety of places at appointed times and owners know when to bring their animals. We also have to try to match our schedules with an owner's working day. In this way, we are actually able to administer to the needs of far more animals to the greater convenience of their owners and this encourages them to use our services. However, at the time of my visit, the clinic's original site was still safe and we spent a wonderful time there, just watching.

Luxor clinic, supporters on a later visit

We shall leave Egypt now, but I shall bring you back. My first visit, as you can tell, was a life-changing experience for someone who had never really travelled much beyond Watford! I returned with a renewed vigour of commitment and a much greater understanding of how it really was – for the animals and for our staff working to help them and their impoverished owners.

The Computer and other seeds of change

It is now 1988. Richard Searight had already been trying to modernise our office practices. He insisted that we have a franking machine. Why? Joan and I were very happy with our damp sponge. But when Richard was onto something, nothing would stand in his way. And it was rather fun using the machine. Then he decided that we should mechanise our typing and bought a huge "word processor", which was kept in the second office and on which we now had to type our list of donors published in the Annual Report. Everyone was listed, with their donations, unless they asked to be anonymous. Joan and I kept these records carefully hand-written onto record cards, and some of them were even multiple and colour coded for banker's orders, deeds of covenant and various types of donation. I recall that we only ever had two complaints that the information published was incorrect. I never really got the hang of that monster word processor. Anyway, it was soon superseded by the dreaded computer.

Richard is a computer buff. And he had found the perfect man to build a programme to fit our needs. But there was one minor problem: Richard didn't know what our needs were. Deeds of covenant, the precursor to Giftaid, were very complicated. Also, every card in the system bore endless little notes about the person – the name of their dog, cat or horse; whether they grew chrysanths; when their husband died and, most importantly, when they first started to donate. We had records going back to 1957, which was when the card system was instigated. Of course, many supporters had been giving for decades even before then. We knew whether their donation was by cheque or banker's order. How would all this be computed? Richard assured us that it would all be alright. There were times when Joan simply had to take a walk around the block and I know it was one of my "going grey" periods.

Well, the new system was designed; the computers were installed. We hired a temp to transfer all the records. But we insisted that we keep the record cards and I sincerely hope that we still have them carefully locked away somewhere. I consider those cards to be a very important part of our history. One lady wrote to me recently and mentioned that she had been supporting us since 1956 and I remembered her name from those cards, many of which I knew intimately! Some of the names amused me because the spelling wanted to defy its pronunciation – like Mr Onions – pronounced Ohnyons; and Mrs De'Ath. Thank Heavens for the apostrophe! Unfortunately, our new computer could only record the names and addresses and the date and amount of the donation. What about all those helpful notes? What about covenanted donations? Again, Joan had to take a walk round the block and I went a little greyer. Actually, it took years for us to get the covenanted donations recorded to our satisfaction. Now we have a system which adds the right amount to the donor's record and at the same time we can produce a list at the touch of a button for the Taxman. Before this happy time, it was all done manually. I know all about that!

I produced the report for Her Majesty's Inspector of Taxes each year, once Joan had retired. Occasionally, we would receive a spot-check visit from on high. If a mistake was found, we would not be allowed to claim the tax on anything, so it was imperative that accuracy prevailed. An Inspector Called, J.B. Priestley-like, one year. He was quite chatty. Yes, he also loved animals and kept snakes as a hobby. For some reason, I looked down at his shoes – grey snakeskin. I would never trust a man who wore grey shoes, but his own snakeskin as well? (I have to record that I've since rescinded my mens' grey shoes opinion. Of necessity...... no names, no packdrill!)

Getting the computer right was taking months. But perhaps we should also remember that ours was one of the first databases to include a word-processing facility – we could "humanise" the system. Richard Searight worked very hard to create a software package that would bridge the transfer from our coloured cards to a computer. In 1989 there was nothing available "off the shelf" for small offices, let alone small charities with very specific requirements. Over time, Richard created a database which became the envy of our sister animal welfare charities. He once timed his wife, Julia, finding a record, entering a donation, creating a receipt, printing a personalised letter and an address label. The computer work took 27 seconds!

Meantime, Richard had made a wonderful film of the Brooke's work (the one we first showed at the House of Commons). He was in his element! He had brought in a very good professional film-making team, who had a great feel for the drama and exotic nature of our work and its locations. We now had something to show people. But, at around the same time, we had begun to get a few phone calls from agitated people asking us whether we still existed. After all, they had left us a legacy and really needed to know. Good Heavens! What was all this about? Had something gone wrong?

Well, apparently, the Daily Mail had published a piece about a deceased lady who had left £10,000 to a charity which no longer existed. That charity was none other than us! But her professional legal executor hadn't done his homework. The lady had left her legacy to the Old War Horse Memorial Hospital. That was our very first name – Mrs Brooke's commemoration of the Cairo Hospital to the memory of those poor old war horses left behind to a fate worse than death by the British Army, after the First World War. The name had later been changed to the Brooke Hospital for Animals (Cairo) and later still (Cairo) was dropped. Each of these changes had been reported to the Charity Commission, which makes sure that the origins of a charity can be traced and identified. This was a mistake which could have serious consequences for the Brooke. Richard Searight immediately rang the newspaper and told them to publish a correction, or else! They duly did. It was tiny. No-one would notice it. Richard insisted on a larger correction or legal action would follow. That did the trick.

Not only did the Daily Mail publish a more noticeable notice, it was even noticed – by a woman who had just returned from a holiday in Egypt. She had been to the Brooke clinic at Luxor and had been very impressed. So that little correction leapt out at her. Her interest was aroused and she contacted Richard. It just so happened that the woman in question was Mo Bowyer, a television producer for the BBC! I'm convinced that Higher Management had something to do with this…! The lady's particular programme was the "40 Minutes" series, which covered a variety of subjects each week. I'm sure some of our supporters will remember this series. Richard showed her his new film and she became convinced that she had the makings of a very dramatic documentary. The programme "Cairo Vets" was duly made and televised and then shown not once more, but four more times! Richard took the unprecedented step of spending £30,000 on advertising to coincide with the broadcasts, including in the Radio Times. He also took another unprecedented step: he insured all the advertising, just in case the programme was broadcast on a different day!

Overnight – actually, over two weeks - our supporter list grew from a mere 4,000 to more than 17,000. Can you imagine what that meant on the ground? Well, on the floor. Lots and lots of mail. Six overflowing sacks filled our two little offices. And that computer system certainly came into its own, I grudgingly have to admit. We were able to "capture" the names and addresses and donations of all the new people. Unfortunately, we were not yet able to send thank-you letters, and the monumental task of responding to everyone with our handwritten receipts was taken on by Joan and Lynne and dozens of willing and wonderful volunteer supporters who came into the office and perched on the edge of desks or sat on the floor opening the mail and writing the receipts. We employed a temp to record everything on our now welcome friend, the computer. Now, whenever we see a supporter who joined in 1989 in response to an advert, we know they saw the programme. But it was a stressful time. More grey hair….. We thought we should never get to the bottom of those sacks and for Joan it was the last straw. Her husband had just retired and she decided to follow his footsteps. Things were changing and she felt it was time to go. Not immediately, but in June the following year.

"Cairo Vets" proved to mark a turning point in the history of the Brooke and also in my own career with the charity. Back in 1982 when I joined the staff, there were three of us part-time, we had around 3,000 supporters, three clinics in Egypt and our annual income was in the region of £300,000. The "law of three" was going to change radically.

Chapter Two

FROM THE OLD MILLENIUM TO THE NEW

My first visit to Jordan

The year 2000 didn't just signal the end of a millennium. Much more important than that! It signalled the beginning of a new phase in the development and expansion of the Brooke Hospital for Animals.

The Brooke clinic, Wadi Musa

We were already in Cairo, Alexandria, Luxor and Aswan. We had also opened a beautiful clinic in Edfu. Then in 1988 Princess Alia of Jordan had asked us to open a clinic at the World Heritage Site of Petra, to serve the small community of horses and donkeys that work so hard in the tourist trade there. Although Petra turned out to be our most expensive area of operation per horse capita, it nevertheless was remarkably good at attracting new Brooke supporters. On the site of a world-famous and popular tourist location, it was an ideal showcase for our work on a small scale. Petra also proved to be a popular destination for Brooke supporters and we organised several highly successful tours to Jordan.

Let me take you there.

I shall never forget my first sight of the little clinic on the other side of the small valley known as Wadi Musa – the Valley of Moses. A rocky, almost white landscape, interrupted by the young green trees which we had planted, provided a backdrop for the series of small, low buildings comprising the clinic and shade shelters for the animals to rest beneath between jobs, the horses looking rather vulnerable in relation to the scale of their surroundings. And vulnerable indeed they were. Galloped mercilessly over the uneven, stony terrain, the horses frequently had damaged knees and legs, and the donkeys were regularly overladen by "weight-challenged" tourists.

In Egypt, Richard Searight had earlier instigated the idea of a competition for the best kept horse and gharry in Luxor, to instil a sense of pride in the owners. It was a simple but very effective ruse. In Jordan, the competitive nature of the horse owners didn't need much encouragement to prove the worth of their steeds and Richard soon introduced the competition to Petra. However, the locals took it a stage further, with a very exciting race before the final judging took place.

On my first trip, we were privileged to have our royal patron, Princess Alia, to preside over the judging. Princess Alia made an excellent judge, since she herself owned a very fine Arab stud. In fact, one of the highlights of a supporter tour to Jordan was the visit to Princess Alia's Royal Stud. I still have a mental picture of one of our party who was a professional artist, sketch book in hand, and looking very much the part under her straw sunhat, as though she had stepped out of the pages of *A Diary of an Edwardian Lady*. Our supporter then sold the paintings she later worked up from her sketches of the Princess's horses prancing round the arena and had cards printed from them, all in aid of the Brooke. I am lucky to have an original on my wall.

Back to Petra and the race. The race and judging always took place in an area near Wadi Musa known as Petra Beida (Little Petra), which was open and wide and relatively stone-free. The

The line-up

scenery was dramatic, with towering cliffs in the distance. Before the race, to build up the excitement and momentum and generally have a good time, the men would dance and sing in traditional style and we would be milling about, taking photos with increasingly dust-filled cameras. Then the men would mount their horses and line up. What anticipation! What excitement! Goodwood? No comparison! The horses were beautifully decorated and the men dressed to the hilt with belts and buckles and head-dresses flying in the wind.

Richard started the race. Starting the race was rather like being at an auction - if you scratch your nose, you have bought the Ming vase for several thousand over your budget. One false move of Richard's hand, or head, would immediately be interpreted as the signal to start – by some, if not all. And the over-eager ones would reluctantly have to return to the starting line.

Petra Beida, dramatic backdrop

I have no doubt that one of the Bedouin would have willingly provided Richard with a starting rifle, if he'd asked. But he didn't and had to resort to a manual signal. Finally, after a few false starts, a signal was clearly conveyed. And they're off! The spectacle of thirty or even fifty or more horses racing across the desert amid clouds of dust, with the backdrop of rocky cliffs, the sand in your face and your camera, the wind in the horses' manes and their riders' headgear had to be seen to be believed. It was so exciting, like a scene from "*Lawrence of Arabia*". It was usually known beforehand who would be the winner of the race. A done deal. But everyone returned, exhilarated and laughing, proud of their performance, ready to line up and wait for the royal judgement. Princess Alia was superb. Natural and friendly, yet always dignified and in command.

The next day, it would be back to work for those magnificent horses. But the little donkeys toiling in the main tourist areas never got to shine, only to sweat. All those steps up to the High Places and the Monastery. The Brooke staff was always on the case, trying to ensure that they were cared for appropriately.

But it was a struggle convincing the young teenage boys who looked after them.

Richard's responsibility on the supporters' tour was to organise the race and ensure that the vets were well prepared for the visitors. Mine was to organise the supporters! As the Brooke representatives, the smooth running of each day, the personal comfort of the supporters, the timing of events and answering questions about the work were ultimately Richard's and my shared responsibility. Getting everyone together at the same time wasn't always the easiest task. On this particular trip, the oldest member of our group must have been quite a knock-out when she was younger. She still wore her hair long and blonde and, in her safari suit and mascara, she looked as though she had just stepped off the *African Queen*. She was a well-enhanced eighty-plus who always smoked her cigarette in an elegant holder. If we couldn't find her, I knew she would be lurking behind a hotel pillar, having a last drag on a fag. One day, we were visiting an archaeological site and had to pick our way over some tricky bits. I saw our blonde bombshell ahead and went up to her and offered her my arm. Not missing a beat, she said, "Why, do you need help, dear?"

As well as organising supporter tours, the London office also had to get all the supplies for the clinic shipped out to Jordan. I was initially responsible for that, too, though eventually it became the responsibility of Julia Searight, Richard's wife, who had been commandeered on to the Brooke office staff. Because Princess Alia had kindly allowed us to use her "diplomatic bag" to eliminate freight transport charges, this meant being in touch with the Jordanian airline named after her, arranging for delivery of the material to the correct shed at London Airport, arranging for its collection and delivery to her royal stud and finally arranging for its collection by a member of Brooke staff to be taken from the stud to Petra. I also had to place the order with the veterinary supplier in the first place. The course of true shipment never runs smoothly and items did occasionally get lost en route. One was an expensive piece of X-ray equipment. I happened to mention this to a Brooke supporter who did regular business runs to Jordan and Petra at the time. Lo and behold! This kind and generous man bought us a replacement X-ray machine.

As well as medicaments and other veterinary supplies, kind supporters would send us numnahs (horse blankets) which they thought would be helpful for the Jordanian horses in winter. Fortunately, their freight was free, thanks to Princess Alia's "diplomatic bag", otherwise they would have cost us far more than their worth just to send them out. I had to organise their collection from various points in the UK and then their delivery to the right airport shed. In the scheme of memorable Brooke moments, these were legion, as I would discuss the somewhat numbing subject of numnahs - their size, suitability and despatch - at great length with a lot of very generous and well-meaning supporters. But conversing with supporters was always a great experience for me, whatever the subject.

Joan kicks off her shoes and I step into them

Meantime, Joan had retired from the London office and I was in charge! Of the office, that is. Richard had been appointed Organising Secretary, a title which could also be translated as "Director". One of the remarkable aspects of the early days of my working for Brooke was the way it went in tandem with my family commitments. To begin with, I worked from 10 to 2.30, so that I could deliver children to school in the morning and collect them in the afternoon. As they got older and were both at the same school, we gradually moved from the complete chauffeuse routine to being met at the bus stop. All this happened over a period of years as my hours at the office increased to meet the ever-burgeoning workload. So, by the time I took over from Joan and had to become a full-time employee for the first time, my sons were completely independent in their travelling arrangements to and from school. But my day still started at 6 a.m. and ended at midnight.

Although Joan had done a brilliant job keeping the books, and we had also relied on our auditors for advice, the Brooke's expanded horizons signified that a more expanded view of its financial

Staff and Trustees at Panton Street office, Major Philip Searight in foreground

management was now necessary. The first task after Joan's departure was to find a reliable book-keeper. I was only reliable if the window was on the debit side and the door was on the credit side, because that's how it was at secretarial college. I would be completely thrown if the layout of the room differed in any way. Thank goodness, we found Captain David Nash, a highly competent management accountant. David was able to present meaningful financial data to the Trustees He set up the systems, provided the tools and applied his craft with vigour and rigour.

There were now six of us using the two small offices in British Columbia House –four of us who were there every day, plus Richard, who came in two or three days a week (with Julia assisting him at home the other two days), and Colonel Brian Thompson, who had just been appointed as our Director. He succeeded Richard, who could concentrate on that at which he was so talented – fundraising and meeting supporters. Brian had previously headed the Royal Army Veterinary Corps and had initially been taken on as a consultant to review our entry into India, which had not been going smoothly. Pakistan had also been drawn to our attention as being very needy.

Something had to happen soon to accommodate everyone. I found the perfect offices overlooking Leicester Square. It had windows opening onto "fresh" air, fireplaces to give character, a very low rent and virtually nil rates. I had my own office which had an alarm bell to ward off the perils of working in central London and though the lift didn't always work, everything else did. For a while, at least….

More space, more staff

Joshua blew his trumpet and all the walls came tumblin' down. It was quite a moment. Most of us lost our offices for the sake of the great expansion that was taking place in the work overseas which, as always, had repercussions in the amount of work generated in the London office. We had to manage such expansion, raise the funds for it, procure and mobilise staff for it and **accommodate** the whole management package which comes with an expanded force. A couple of people did keep their personal space but I wasn't one of them. Changes came thick and fast; as we progressed overseas, so changes came to our management structure and work environment at home. It was all unsettling but very good for the ego! And if one kept one's focus on the animals, the wonderful people who were one's colleagues at home and abroad, and the not-to-be-sniffed-at fact that one had a pay-cheque coming in each month, then it was all so easy....

And where were we expanding to? Well, Brooke in Pakistan was opening up centres around the original hub established in Peshawar and also in Lahore. (I shall tell you more later about our setting up in Pakistan). India was definitely now moving in the right direction with the right management, and its teams were reaching further and further afield from Delhi. More teams were working in Egypt and we had started to work with an NGO in Afghanistan. One day, the head of that particular organisation came to London. I was the only one who could understand him! His English was so heavily disguised by his accent that any dialogue with him was accompanied by some consternation. But, for some reason, I guessed my way along as he spoke and was invariably correct, at least it appeared so because he always beamed gratefully in my direction.

And of course we had to expand our fundraising activity to keep pace. This was where the fun began. For instance, who remembers a campaign called 'Courses for Horses'? This was a brilliant title invented to cover our "infiltration" of the racing fraternity. For a whole year, our staff scoured the country attending events, races and generally meeting the high and mighty of the racing world. Our old friend, Sir Peter O'Sullevan, was such a great help here, with introductions, opening doors – and gates – and great ideas. I went to Goodwood for the first time. Unfortunately, it was freezing cold. I remember marvelling at our sex's ability to ignore any violation of the senses in terms of heat or cold for the sake of "the look". Bravo! Our supporters were brilliant and caught the spirit of it all, helping at events, creating their own. But it was hard work and we couldn't keep up the momentum for more than a year on the staff resources we had then.

Our new fundraising director, John Trampleasure, liked to keep his staff feeling happy and valued, so he inaugurated the "away day" – a day away from the office when we could bond with each other, playing strange games to prove our ingenuity and team spirit, sharing our department's work and news, trials and tribulations, and, well, bonding….. On one of these, we had just heard a rather long discourse from a colleague and I could feel that the energy barometer was falling fast. *Zzzzzzz!* So, when she finished, I said to my dear boss, "I think we need a change of activity for a moment, John." He looked at me nervously, sensing something was in the offing, and said, "Oh no!" So I did it, anyway. I got up and sang a snappy little number from the 30s, twinkling round the table to the sound of laughter and clapping. It did the trick!

But I can hear some of you say "That's enough of office life. We want to know more about your moments with the animals." In my defence, most of my time with the Brooke was spent in the office! However, over a period of 28 years, I made thirteen overseas trips, ten of them with supporters. I also spent time travelling around the UK, visiting supporters. So, in the following chapters, I promise to reveal some more riveting Brooke moments from those overseas trips.

Chapter Three

MORE VIGNETTES FROM OVERSEAS

Oh, those trips! There were so many moments of sadness, of hope, of achievement and of light bulbs going on, so many moments of humour and companionship, so many moments of sheer delight. I have allowed myself to go with the flow of my memory here, as I bring forward some outstanding moments, which may not necessarily be painted in orderly consecutiveness, but hopefully in rich colours.

Jordan…again

Petra Clinic seen from the stony path to the Siq

Following the success of two earlier trips to Jordan, we organised a third for our intrepid supporters. It was a popular destination and we had at the time an expert English company to guide us. The proprietors of the company were also very staunch Brooke supporters, so it gave them a chance to see the work for themselves and promote the Brooke on their other tours.

In Jordan, we were making some inroads with the bedouin horse owners but their animals were still a problem. It was almost always the boys who caused the trouble. The youngsters would try to compete with each other and no matter how many times we told them to stop racing the animals across the stony terrain, they would just cock a rude snoop at our staff and carry on. It did take quite a while to get the parents to instil some discipline into these unruly youngsters.   We have radically altered our approach over the years and it is now the very horse owners who are running the clinic! What a turnaround! We are delighted. We maintain a veterinary presence and are on hand for emergencies. But this most expensive of our operations is now financed by the Jordanian Tourist Authority in Petra.

Bedouin tent

However, at the time of this third trip, the Brooke was still entirely responsible for running the clinic it had established.

If you've never been to Petra "the rose red city half as old as time", you should put it on your list.   After the first glimpse of the little Brooke clinic on the hillside opposite the banks of hotels, some of which had sprung up newly and hopefully when the border between Jordan and Israel opened up, you are taken along a narrow gorge between towering cliffs of pink and grey and brown. You can go on horseback, by horse-drawn carriage, by donkey or by my favourite - Shanks's Pony. I always relied on my shanks. It took quite a while to reach the first of the historic sites, the Treasury, but I always enjoyed the slow walk, looking at the striations of rose, grey and olive brown rocks, following the old Roman drainage channels on either side, and peering into some of the caves where the Bedouin used to live.   Just imagine even earlier inhabitants and visitors in Roman togas, walking the same route, while they discussed the latest news and trade from across the Empire.

The manager of our clinic, Mohammad Hilalat, had been the last bedou of his family to have been brought up in a cave. It had been a thriving, happy community. The people also used to live in tents of woven wool. This material was perfect because it expanded with the damp winter air to keep out the cold and then became aerated and cool in the heat of summer.

Mohammad very sweetly wrote a poem in Arabic into my journal. It is "*From a Bedouin Princess*" and reads thus: "*A tent with winds blowing - it is more lovely to me than a big spacious palace.*" But the local authorities, with the tourist trade in mind, didn't like the look of the smoke-blackened caves and rocks or the paraphernalia inevitably associated with human habitation, so everyone was moved into concrete boxes called "new houses", each one with its own door and fluorescent lighting. Unlike the tents, they are badly insulated - hot in the summer and cold in the winter.

The best time of day to start an excursion is some time before sunrise, depending on your mode of travel. Then you will arrive at the Treasury just when the dawning sun strikes its pink rock into an incandescent glow. It looks lit from within. The first sight of this amazing feat of human endeavour and artistry is vertical, narrow, long and stunning.   It has inspired artists like David Roberts and, more latterly, our own Brooke supporter, the late Derek Pearson. (Derek donated his version of this iconic view for us to use as a bookmark for supporters.) You are treated to just a glimpse as you approach the end of the gorge and the rocks gradually open out. It moved me to tears the first time I saw it. The space becomes enormous as you make your slow approach, and the scale of the buildings all hewn out of the cliffs is awe-inspiring.   The intricacy of the decoration beggars belief. Around the huge entrances are gathered diminutive people, camels, horses and traders. The quiet of the place is spellbinding and it is as though everything is happening in slow motion.

A glimpse of sunrise in the Siq

Some of us decide to climb to the High Places. There are over 800 steps to this place of sacrifice. It is on top of the world, it seems to me, as I sit there, tracing my finger along the channel cut in the rock floor for the sacrificial blood to run away. Black silky goats have no trouble at all in beating me to the top. Little do they know how lucky they are that I work for the Brooke, that I have no sacrificial motive in being in this place. Little do they know what a hard time their more unfortunate ancestors had of it, being offered up to appease or thank or implore. In spite of its ancient bloody reputation, the High Places is still the quietest spot on earth that I have ever experienced. The sky is deep, deep blue, cloudless and empty of any trespass, either feathered or metal. I feel I can sit for hours and hours, drinking in the silence, out of time. This is where my "holiday" takes place – my holy day.

Although I knew the manager of the clinic quite well from my previous visits, I had not met his assistant, Hussein. I had that pleasure later in the day, when we discussed the work and the difficulties with the boys but he really wanted to tell me about his six-year-old daughter. I made an exchange - told him about my young sons. I thought nothing more of it when I left. I was due to have dinner with the manager, Mohammad Hilalat, and his family. In their home. This was a great honour and I wasn't sure what to expect. I remembered this time to tell him that I didn't eat meat. You don't eat meat? Not any meat? Mohammad couldn't imagine life without it.

The time came and I was picked up and taken to Mohammad Hilalat's house (sadly, he has since passed away). And I wasn't prepared for the welcome: it was overwhelming. The whole family was there – uncles, aunts, cousins, Mohammad's many children and his lovely wife. Did I speak any Arabic? None! So Mohammad was my mouthpiece. Mohammad had to work very hard as there was so much to say. I particularly chimed with his wife, as we had children the same age.

With all this animated conversation, I was getting hungrier and hungrier. The sun had set hours ago and I wondered whether I would be eating that night. Then, to my surprise, everyone except the immediate family suddenly got up, said goodbye and left. And Mohammad announced it was now time for supper and led me to a room at the back of the house. This room had no furniture but a brightly coloured tablecloth was spread on the floor, surrounded by cushions against the walls. It was covered with all sorts of dishes, the centrepiece of which was a cold omelette and cold potato chips. Thank you so much.......You *have* made something vegetarian. Mohammad motioned me to sit on a cushion and then he and his wife and children left the room. I was all alone with a tablecloth spread to its circumference with food. Mohammad! Come back! What have I said? But, apparently, the honoured guest is always invited to partake of the food first and the host and hostess politely eat the leftovers (just as Brigadier Sami had done in Egypt all those years ago). I couldn't be doing that. So I remonstrated and said that in the Brooke we are all family and I really want everyone to eat with me. I so appreciate the honour but I would enjoy my evening with them even more if they did me the honour of eating with me. Put like that, how could they refuse? They accepted my invitation and honour was satisfied.

After supper, Mohammad said that he would take me to Hussein, his assistant, for coffee. Well, that was a surprise and not in the plan. I was thinking of my early morning schedule with supporters and it was already at least 10.00 p.m. But the young Hussein had insisted on extending hospitality to me. He was not going to be outdone by his boss. Little did I know how far he would go to impress….

I was greeted at his door by Hussein and immediately taken through a room which appeared almost empty except for a glazed cupboard immediately to my left and a wash basin set into the wall by some stairs in the far corner. We went up the stairs and into a large room which almost covered the entire first floor. It had a wonderful Lurex three-piece suite and lots of cushions, with a coffee table in the centre. I was impressed, as I knew how much we paid Hussein!! I was seated in a huge armchair and we started to talk. Then Hussein snapped his fingers at nothing in particular and from a door at the far end, a beautiful child entered. This was Hussein's six-year-old daughter. She was carrying lots of things in her arms. She came and sat next to me. We said hello to each other and then Hussein said she had some presents for me and my sons. I was shocked and became acutely embarrassed as I had come empty-handed, not being prepared for this visit. My embarrassment had only just begun, however.

Firstly, I was presented with a flag to commemorate King Hussein's birthday, then a St Christopher pendant on a chain, then a little box, then a full-sized prayer mat and other things which I can't even remember. Then this very confident little six-year-old gave me an envelope addressed to Mrs Lynne's sons. She had written them a letter in English! No wonder Hussein wanted me to come and visit! He wanted me meet his Jordanian princess. But how to respond to such generosity? My face was getting redder and redder. I could feel the blush at the roots of my hair. So I just let the tears fall, which they wanted to do.

After the presentation, Hussein again snapped his fingers and two women appeared with coffee for us all. These were his wife and her sister. Not being used to Arab ways with their womenfolk, I was inwardly getting redder and redder at the finger-snapping, too. I made a huge fuss of the women and tried to direct all the conversation towards them, via Mohammad and Hussein. Then it was time to go.

We left by the route we had come, down the stairs and across the empty downstairs room. This time, I could see the vitrine filled with objects. I went up to it on my way to the door and made one of the biggest mistakes of my life. I admired its contents. That was a Brooke moment I shall never forget. I didn't know at the time that if you tell an Arab you like his shoes, he will give them to you, if you admire his Lurex cushions, he will present them to you. Immediately, the doors of the vitrine were opened and the entire shelves were cleared into my hands. All their little objects of desire which they had bought, shards of Roman pottery which they had discovered, pieces of rock they had collected, were all placed into bags and given to the woman who didn't keep her mouth closed.

Then the tears really flowed. I didn't know where to put myself. My hosts were kindness itself and I went away with a completely new understanding of generosity. Although I admit that I don't always immediately give away the jewellery or clothes which someone might admire, I know that this experience truly opened my heart to a new level of giving to which I could aspire and practise in my own life.

Egypt…again

Mares with their foals in the open air

During my second visit to Egypt, this time with supporters, I discovered an important device which I could use to good effect whenever I was with a horse or donkey that needed treatment. My own voice! And the audience turned out to be highly appreciative, regardless!

Our arrival at the Cairo Hospital was a wonderful Brooke moment for me. I had not been since my first visit in 1988 with my husband. This was now 1994. I was welcomed like family. Mustapha, the driver, welcomed me like an old friend. Indeed, the entire party was welcomed like this. It was red carpet all the way. We had a wonderful time being shown around the various buildings and open areas. The inmates were given such care and attention in their individual stalls and, once they were ready, they could recuperate in the open areas outside.

The mares and stallions were kept separate and some mares had their little foals with them.

Supporters and staff outside the Hospital in Cairo

They stayed there for some time, to make sure that the foals weren't put to work too early. Not every owner could be persuaded but it was already a mark of the influence of the Brooke that this was becoming the custom.

The Cairo Hospital was crowded with visitors being shown around all the stalls and this change in the usually tranquil atmosphere naturally had an effect on some of the inmates. There was one horse who was particularly upset. I suddenly had the notion that singing a Sanskrit mantra would do the trick.

I approached the horse and stood a little way off, chanting the words very softly and, I hoped, sweetly. I moved nearer, very slowly, and the magic of sound did its work. The horse calmed down. I was amazed at this new horse-whispering technique I had discovered. After that, there was no stopping me. Whenever I met an animal, I quietly sang into its ear. I must have looked very strange from behind and no-one knew what I was doing. At least, so I thought.

Then, lunch at the British Embassy was amazing. The gracious, spacious rooms, the quiet attendance to our needs by the staff, the delicious food and the warm air wafting around stately columns was a stark contrast to the experiences of the morning. The Embassy had always taken an interest in the work of the Hospital. Indeed, that was how the late Lady Weir, Hilary Weir, came to be involved and ultimately became a Trustee and Chairman of the Board. Her husband had been the British Ambassador in Egypt in the late 70s and she had arranged fund-raising events for us at the Embassy during his tour of duty.

A British trustee also on this trip, Judi Payne, and I went with Dr Nagi to a stock market on the edge of town. Although we passed through what appeared to be green belt fields within the city, the market itself was situated between tall tenement blocks. There was a large area in the centre covered by awning and a group of men were smoking hookahs. These were the rich camel owners. Apparently, if you owned five camels, you were rich. Further along were the donkey owners. These men seemed to me to be rougher, coarser, and definitely poorer. The donkeys were grouped according to their condition – good, mediocre and *** awful. Judi and I were distressed by some that we saw. There were three in particular which Nagi wanted to buy for destruction. One had his chain noseband completely embedded in his flesh and looked utterly debilitated. We were the only women in the area, of course. We didn't realise until later that our presence influenced the owners' asking price as they thought we would pay more. Nagi was good-natured with them and, with the help of an independent negotiator who happened to come along, we did manage to buy the one with the noseband. Dr Nagi had been impressive during these negotiations: quiet, authoritative, unafraid, even joking with the men. Meantime, Judi and

I, standing a way off once we realised we weren't helping the situation, were surrounded by a mob of young boys who teased us. We weren't to come to any real harm but I did feel uneasy

Alexandria Clinic courtyard viewed from roof

and certainly would not have wanted to be there alone. We took our little chap back to the hospital. On the way, Nagi always had his eyes peeled and stopped twice to treat a couple of horses.

Our trip included a visit to Alexandria. The clinic at Alexandria is so charming. All its buildings are painted white and, at the time of my visit, it was enhanced with bright red geraniums.

The work there is often focused on the horses working around the dockland areas and the animals suffer greatly from throat and bronchial complaints due to the damp, foggy air. A pair of horses was waiting to be shod outside the clinic. They reminded me of the two old pals who were never parted in Mrs Brooke's original Cairo stable and whom we still honour by always including their photo in our newsletters. The more decrepit one almost leaned on his stronger companion for support. I stood by them for ages, chanting my meditation mantra quietly to them. I did get some strange looks. However, both horses moved closer and closer to listen, until, finally, one poor friend's nose rested on my chest. (I'm rather glad that I don't have that effect on all my audiences when I sing…) Anyway, his owner looked astonished and said to me, "He talk you?!!" I nodded, since I couldn't match his English with my Arabic. The horses and I, however, could certainly speak the same language.

One day, in Aswan, a small group of us took time out to visit St. Simeon's Monastery. After a peaceful trip on a felucca, we disembarked for the next stage of our journey. I was feeling not a little trepidation about the forthcoming camel ride. I had changed into a Punjabi outfit, plus sunhat and chiffon scarf. With scarf enveloping my head, I was told I looked like Freya Stark! The camels loomed large and I asked for a slow one, not realising that they were all slow. I thought I would be riding side-saddle for some reason but, in the event, it was definitely "leg-over". This wasn't easy for one as stiffly unprepared as me. Once on top, it was like being in a swaying armchair. We walked in stately procession up an incline strewn with rocks. After a little while I decided I loved my camel! I also loved the old man walking by its side. He had cared for this animal and I felt cared for by both of them. I also felt that God had truly cared for the camel – look how He had fashioned his feet! Perfect for the job! All soft and velvety round the rocks and deep in the sand. My camel then spoke and I was reminded of one of the cantors in the Arabic chant which accompanies Dervish turners: the sound was pure and low and came from deep within the body, not the throat. I felt totally exhilarated.

But then it was time to dismount. Hmm….. My singing mount suddenly knelt in obeisance to his owner's command and I lurched forward very ungracefully, considering I was a Freya Stark look-alike. I fell into the arms of the old man, who looked unbelievably embarrassed by this contact with Freya's upper regions. Poor man! I thanked him and embarrassment was dissolved miraculously by the grubby notes which I hastily pressed into his hand.

It was then a short walk to the monastery. The sky was cloudless. There were sun-bleached boulders and rocks strewn about in the sand. This was desert. We were met by a guide who, unhelpfully, spoke almost no English. However, his skill in mime was equal to that of Marcel Marceau. He showed us round the remains, explaining in mime what each area would have been used for – dormitories, refectory, etc. When he came to the latrines, we were given the full works, complete with sound effects. We entered St Simeon's cell, where the monk used to pray and meditate every day. There was a large iron ring embedded into the low ceiling. Before commencing his long hours of prayer, St Simeon would knot his long hair through the ring. If he nodded off, the ring would bring him efficiently, though sharply, back in focus. I personally think a sofa is a better option.

The carriage competition

Judi Payne and I are about the same age but she, even in those days, was prematurely grey. As we walked along the Luxor Corniche together, a man came up to her and offered to pay her 40 camels for her daughter! Since we had only recently heard that five camels indicated richesse, I thought this was a bit over the top. Anyway, she wasn't sure where she could keep them all happily in her Northumberland garden, so she declined.

One of Richard Searight's most efficacious institutions was the carriage horse competition. He instituted this in Luxor as a means to encourage better horse husbandry from the carriage drivers who plied for trade along the Corniche. Anyone who has been to Luxor or Aswan will remember the discomfort they will have felt when being raced along the road at breakneck speed by a malnourished or poor old horse. Many will have refused to use a carriage if the horse was in this state of health. There is a huge element of competition among the drivers – speed, shiny brass decorations on the carriage. Richard thought he would harness this competitive spirit (please forgive the pun!) and turn it to the advantage of the horses themselves.

I have attended a number of Richard's competitions. They were quite grand and exciting affairs. There is always an air of expectancy as everyone gathers under a colourful printed canopy, with

Lynne about to present rosettes to Luxor carriage competition winners

soft drinks a-plenty, waiting for the Mayor of Luxor to arrive (sometimes waiting for what seems like hours). All the drivers are lined up ready to drive round the circuit. They have been preparing for the day for some months. No-one is allowed to enter the competition if their horse is not up to scratch in every way or has not been in good condition for many months prior to the competition. Regular inspections take place beforehand to make sure everyone abides by the rules. On the occasion I now recall, we all sat in our places waiting for the Mayor. And then we were told that he had something urgent come up and sent his apologies. So yours truly was asked to hand out the rosettes. This was such an honour and pleasure. I can't tell you how good it was to see the expression of delight on the face of each winner. All the horses looked magnificent. Judi was the judge since she was a renowned equine writer and journalist in her day job. And the brasses winked and shone brassily in the sunshine. The paintwork on each carriage was immaculate and the men looked clean and handsome in their flowing galabyahs.

Luxor gharry with Brooke staff member Raghib

India

My visit to India in 2003 was so inspiring. I was on my own, having spent some time in an ashram near Mumbai, and afterwards went to update myself on Brooke's work in and around Delhi, just for a couple of days.

Brigadier Rappai in foreground; Colonel Pundir in background with staff member

We had started in India some years before and the work was now being taken forward with great vim and vigour by Brigadier Rappai and Colonel Pundir and their amazing team of highly-motivated and laterally-thinking staff.

Everything was fit for purpose – the modest, clean and well-equipped suburban house which served as the Brooke India headquarters; the neat and tidy laboratory and medicine storeroom (even the last needle had to be accounted for and no-one was allowed to cross the threshold to help himself to supplies); and the shade shelters at the tonga stands, simply made from bamboo, tarpaulin and wood by the tonga owners themselves. I saw how the idea of appointing local people as community welfare workers really had taken off. One young man in his Brooke apparel and his box of tricks was so proud to show off his newly acquired skills.

Harness-maker at work

I remember going to one tonga stand – a considerable drive out of Delhi into Uttar Pradesh. We had secured an area and covered it with thatch for shade and concreted the floor. There were brightly-coloured animal welfare posters all over the place and I could hear the radio going quite loudly, playing music interspersed with speaking. Apparently, these were welfare training messages being meted out to a captive audience. At the back of the stand there was a Brooke-trained harness maker showing men how to mend harnesses with bits of old leather. At that time, we were contributing 50% to the cost of this. I was amazed to learn that, since this very simple innovation had been introduced, harness galls had dropped dramatically.

Brooke India is always looking for simple, practical solutions to problems. For instance, at a tonga stand under a fly-over, Brooke India arranged to have the ground concreted so that the horses would be standing on dry ground. This simple innovation greatly improved the condition of their hooves.

Lynne after chai surrounded by her hosts

We drove on to a vast brick kiln which I recognised as having been featured in a ground-breaking Dutch television programme about our work. Since I have mentioned the Dutch, I shall digress for a moment to the Netherlands, where a very strong supporter group had been so successful in their fund-raising efforts, that managing the burgeoning Dutch supporters was becoming a full-time job for the volunteers. We therefore established a Dutch Trust to take advantage of local charity tax breaks and to employ paid staff. Over the years, the Dutch team has been extremely successful in raising awareness and funds. One of its successes was to secure a television company to make a programme about our work in India, and this is the programme to which I refer.

Dr Thannimal with supporter

In the brick kiln there was such an air of desolation to greet us, and the penetrating wind blew red dust everywhere. One of our staff was going to show a training video which had been shot at that kiln and we all squashed into someone's dark little brick house. Even the women came out of hiding. There was a great deal of hilarity and elbow nudging as they saw themselves on the screen. That was when I was memorably served hot, sweet chai direct from a brick kiln bucket...... When it was all over, our lady vet, Dr. Thannimal, and I exchanged looks and then goodbyes, both of us with tears in our eyes. I remember seeing tears in the eyes of the women as I said goodbye to them, too.

Dr Thannimal is amazingly compassionate with the animals and the people. Both they and her fellow Brooke colleagues always speak so highly of her. Once, on her day off, she drove a young baby suffering from sunburn from its village to hospital quite a long way off and then brought it home again. Dr Thannimal has incredible energy and often works by torchlight. Our vets In India are often invited to family occasions – weddings, funerals, births…

Brick kiln children

I also remember spending a couple of wonderful hours at a huge craft market just on the outskirts of Delhi. It was spread over a vast area and contained all sorts of colourful and well-designed stalls selling the most beautiful artefacts from all over India. And such delicious food…. Those who know me would recognise this as bargain-hunter Lynne's Heaven! Wonderfully made articles at a fraction of the price I would have to pay in the UK. I bought shawls for friends, bits of jewellery, and a beautiful sisal woven mat for my kitchen for a mere £6.50. I only threw it out last year! Fortunately, the remaining space in my suitcase limited Lynne's shopping spree.

Brick kiln water carrier

Another Sanskrit chanting moment, this time in Delhi during the same trip; I was with a mobile team visiting the Police Chowk tonga stand. There was one particular horse having treatment to his eye. I was warned not to go too close as he was known to be unpredictable, with a reputation for irritability and kicking. He could go up in smoke. He certainly looked very restless and was probably in some considerable discomfort. The vet was definitely having some difficulty administering the eye ointment.

After he had received his treatment I stood a few feet in front of him and started to sing softly. His ears moved round like radar antennae, so I carried on, holding my hand near his nose. When I moved forward he shied away. I continued to sing and didn't move a muscle. After a while, his head had gradually dropped so I could sing into his ears and our eyes met. I held his gaze and he moved closer. The siren's magic was working! He became quiet and his nose came to rest on my outstretched hands and his eyes were closing. Eventually, to my great joy, he moved even closer, with his head on my chest, and I rested my head against his. It was remarkable. My own eyes were glistening. I knew this poor creature had never experienced gentleness before. No wonder he was difficult to handle!

More irresistible brick kiln children

I turned round, tears streaming down my cheeks, to face a crowd of men, all of whom, unbeknown to me, had been watching this entire healing episode with great wonder.

[As an aside and a propos of nothing to do with the Brooke, let me share the following with you: I once decided (only once) to sing to a field of cows in Wales. I was on my own in deep country and they were up a hill on the other side of the field. I just let rip! And they all came down to see what the noise was about. They stood in a row in front of me and listened politely for quite a while. Then one of them gave a nod, rather like a disinterested shrug, turned round and went back up the hill. The rest of the audience turned round, one after the other, and followed suit. It obviously wasn't as good as they thought it would be. But at least they didn't ask for their money back.]

From my journal:

India is the place
Where face meets face.
The mutual smile
Lasts for mile after mile.
Eyes are alight
With such generous delight
That seeing God in each other
Is like meeting your love.

India 2007

There was a later trip to India in 2007. It took a great deal of organisation beforehand and amazing organisational skills by our Indian staff. They had mounted a detailed and highly informative exhibition of their work for us to examine during a lunch on our first day. Unfortunately, I had not listened to my own intuition which had told me that this would be too much on the first day of our arrival, though I was assured that we should aim to hit the ground running, to keep the momentum going. I found it difficult to restrain myself from going round the group giving some of them a gentle prod at those moments when they were nodding off during the speeches.

Since we first established ourselves in India there have been many changes and whereas the mobile teams used to drive for long distances from a base in Delhi, at the time of our visit in 2007 they had set up small field offices in seven districts of Western Uttar Pradesh. Each area had its team of one or two veterinary officers, an assistant, a community facilitator and a driver who was also trained in basic veterinary skills and chosen for his natural communication skills. On our first field visit, having divided into small groups as usual, my group attended a regular bi-monthly meeting in Dadri with Dr Saurabh which happened to co-incide with our visit. What stood out for me in this training session was that we, the visitors, were included in the seated circle and when we introduced ourselves to the animal owners, one of our party could say that, as a horse stable owner, he also depended entirely on his horses for his income and if he became ill, he lost his income. It was a memorable unifying moment, when we could sense the recognition in the faces of the local people as the translator spoke.

One memorable moment I have to include did not actually belong to me but was reported by someone in another group. On their way to watch a play about animal care to be put on by the local children, a crate of drinks flew off the roof of their car. The driver calmly reversed into the oncoming traffic on the dual carriageway to pick it up. Indian traffic is quite a circus!

Again, the group as a whole was an interesting assortment of supporters, some of whom had been on previous trips. One had come with her protective brother for company, just in case. Even before we had left Gatwick Airport, she had lost her handbag with her passport and various

other essentials! I recalled Jordan all those years ago, when I might be looking for this lady, only to find her having a calming smoke behind a hotel pillar. But what a stalwart she was – and still is! We are such good friends now that she once sent me a delightful birthday present, beautifully wrapped. As I carefully undid each layer of paper and bows until I was left with a tiny jewellery box, I was filled with trepidation. How could I match such generosity? But I needn't have worried too much. She had kindly sent me a cigarette stub – in memory of the trip! I think her protective brother is still trying to get over it!

Not too sure about this tuk-tuk drive

Our itinerary took in the great Taj Mahal. We took the train from Delhi, and I remember standing on the platform in the cold early morning air, eyeing the occasional rat with some caution. It was the first time I had seen washing hanging out of a train window! My heart did miss a beat when I saw the wondrous sight of the Taj as it floated in the early morning mist. I understood why it is such a cliché for architectural perfection. It deserves to be.

We were then travelling to Jaipur, the long coach journey broken by lunch in a most fabulous old Rajasthani palace. I wandered around its many rooms and gardens, transported into another era, another life.   Once in Jaipur we were scheduled to meet Dr Ashok, who worked for Help in Suffering. The Brooke had worked with this organisation (founded by Christine Townend) for some years and supported Dr Ashok in his work. We parked at a spot in the street and owners started to gather. So did some of the donkeys which were allowed to roam freely in the streets. They tended to follow a leader and if the leader came for treatment, so did all his friends! So the vet's first job was to sort out the wheat from the chaff. After queuing for a while, some donkeys simply walked away! There was an unfortunate case where a brick had fallen on a donkey's leg and it had to be euthanased. Because the animals were left mostly to their own devices, they were very vulnerable and this poor creature had been in considerable pain for three days before its owner had discovered it and called Dr Ashok. It was a tribute to the work and influence of the vet that the owner did call him immediately.

Jaipur is a very beautiful city. Most of the palaces and other important buildings are pink! I felt I was looking at life through rose-tinted glasses….

There is one Brooke moment that will stand out forever from this visit to India. We attended a community training meeting at a local brick kiln. It was extremely dusty, as you would expect. The men sat barefoot on a clean and dust-free carpet. I recognised the carpet not only as a great mark of respect for the training sessions regularly provided by the Brooke but also on this occasion for the overseas visitors. This was sacred space. So there was a moment of embarrassment when I realised that some of the party had put their shoe-clad feet on the carpet, but it was too late. I did ask everyone to remove their shoes if they were touching the carpet but it was a moment when I realised how ill-prepared we were for this meeting of cultures.

I then introduced our group to the men as I often tried to do if the situation allowed. I explained how some of them raised money to help them and their animals. I made it clear that all the money given came from hard-won earnings or as a result of arranging fundraising events or making items to sell. I explained that many of our donors were elderly people on pensions. This not only impressed the animal owners but also our vets and Brooke staff, too. One animal owner asked why we did it. A good question! It led to a lively discussion and a supporter responded that we respected all life, and animals should be treated with respect. Her comment seemed to encapsulate everything perfectly and this theme then became the vet's basis for the training session. The men were asked to list all the ways they could show respect to their animals. One told how much he loved his horse. As he said this, a horse appeared from behind the wall which turned out to be his horse. He went to lead it away and it gave him quite a kick. Everyone laughed because the man had been lying; in reality he apparently treated his animal very badly. Only fools and horses………

Pakistan

I have been to Pakistan three times, twice with supporters, and I long to return. I think it is the surprise of Pakistan that attracts me. I had already met some of the trustees of the Pakistan Board and one or two of the more senior staff visiting the London office. But it wasn't until I went to Pakistan myself that I realised what truly great people the Pakistanis are and how stunningly beautiful is their country. How orderly everything is! The shops display all their wares beautifully, especially the food shops. Bread and cakes, sweets and fruit make a wonderfully colourful pattern of pyramids, circles and ovals. Shopkeepers seem to take pride in the visual attraction of their goods, either inside, outside or hanging from above. In the

countryside, the fields are kept in such good order. Potato crops make a wonderful basket weave design, contrasting with the green of young rice or wheat. In the small towns, pavements and roads are regularly swept clean. The plethora of notices in rural districts denoted quite a hierarchy of local "council" management.

Shops in Gilgit, North West Frontier Province

Before I reminisce about our first supporter trip in Pakistan, one which everyone on it considered to be life-changing, let me tell you how we came to be in Pakistan in the first place.

It was Sandy Gore, television journalist and personality, who first drew our attention to the needs of the pack animals which were traversing the Tribal Territories in the North West Frontier of Pakistan between Afghanistan and Pakistan. This is a no-man's land where tribal law rules. The terrain is harsh and, as our British Army personnel have found out to their cost, very difficult to come to terms with, and very easy to hide away whatever you want to hide away.

One of our trustees, John Brocklehurst, and his life-long friend, Colonel Khushwaqt ul-Mulk, together with Brooke Director, Colonel Brian Thompson, took it upon themselves to see whether there really was a need, as Sandy Gore had indicated, and an opportunity for the Brooke to expand its work. All three gentlemen have since passed away.

They explored the Hindu Khush beyond Peshawar and into the Tribal Territories, this area of Pakistan which is always volatile, unpredictable and fascinating. They wanted to monitor the movement of pack animals over the mountains from Afghanistan. How many? How often? How needy? In the vain hope of being inconspicuous, they decided to dress "native" and camp in the mountains.

Those three must have had a wonderful time, returning to their boyhood scouting adventures camping in the Hindu Khush, while they counted pack animals crossing the mountains from Afghanistan into Peshawar. They were in tribal territory where the gun ruled. They couldn't be interested in the nature of the pack contents and didn't dare risk showing any interest. They were observing only the condition and numbers of animals to see whether a Brooke presence could be justified in that area. Brian has since told me of some of the real dangers of that trip – being shelled as they drove along the road and other exciting happenings.

Col. Brian Thompson enjoying his pipe

However, they did indulge in a bit of disguise, wearing local garb and headgear, the amazing Chitrali woollen hat. Can you imagine Brian Thompson, all kitted out but not willing to give up his very English pipe? And John Brocklehurst, every inch of his tall commanding frame shouting English, English! Brian took this wonderful photo of John, heavily disguised, as you can see, with the other member of "three men in a tent", Colonel Kushwaqt ul Mulk, which conveys their mood - jaunty, cheeky and unabashed. Only Khush would have looked like the real McCoy – because he was!

John Brocklehurst and Col. Khushwaqt ul *Mulk – Chitrali-style*

Colonel Khush (as he was affectionately known) had an amazing fortress high up in the mountainous area known as Chitral where he lived in splendid isolation with one of his wives during the summer months. (He once entertained Diana Princess of Wales there.) During the winter months he resided in Peshawar with his other wife. Every year Khush would return to his beloved spiritual community at Lindisfarne in Scotland, to replenish his soul. Now isn't that something?

We used to exchange long philosophical letters. When he died, one of his sons sent me some of Khush's wise epithets. Here is one written with Khush's capitals: "Man Seeks Everywhere

Heaven Except Within Himself And Therefore Fails To Find It." Khush was totally inspired by the work of the Brooke and set up the first clinic at Peshawar. His army-engendered organisational and leadership skills were invaluable, as was his courage and tenacity, his forthright views and his sense of right and wrong. He was the cornerstone of the newly-emerging Brooke Pakistan.

Col. Khush looking trim in a lady's sunhat

Colonel Khush was already in his eighties when he took over the leadership of our new venture! Eventually, and very reluctantly, he had to hand over the reins. The perfect person to step into the breach was found in the able Farooq Malik. Intelligent, sensitive and organised, he has not only been the conductor of the orchestra, bringing all the parts into harmony, he has also written many of the parts. And, like a true musician, he listens and hears.

At the same time, very much leading from the Chair of the Pakistani Board of Trustees – the leader to take Brooke Pakistan into the future – was the late General Rafi Alum. What a wonderful character he was! Tall and handsome... Educated at Oxford, with an English mother, on hearing him speak you would not be able to tell him from one of his English fellow dons. His wife, Tameez, was charming, beautiful and also talented as an artist. They had an amazing, super-stylish house and stud farm outside Lahore which they always made available to Brooke trip supporters. We were greeted on that first visit with great pomp and ceremony and yet, at the same time, everything was totally relaxed and informal. I remember being helped down from the coach by him like Cinderella arriving at the ball. The servants provided the pomp and Rafi and his wife provided the welcome. Imagine sitting sipping your cocktail in their garden under the stars, or relaxing in their beautiful house, looking at the *objets d'art*, or strolling down to the fence to meet the horses. And then the food….. All in an atmosphere of relaxed refinement. And yet, great tragedy had already struck Rafi and Tameez: one son had been killed in a car accident and another in a polo accident. One needs resilience and dignity to move on from such losses. And these qualities they both had in abundance.

This first supporter trip took place in 1995, not many years after the founding of Brooke Pakistan in 1991, but long before 9/11, before the shock and melodrama and intrigue of that event, and long before all the strife now taking place. The plan was to fly direct to Lahore, where the head office and an establishment of teams operated, then fly to Islamabad (staying in Rawalpindi) from where we would travel along the Karakoram Highway as far as the border with China. We would return to Peshawar to see the work in the original founding clinic and then return home. The trip was in the hands of a reputable UK travel agent whom we had used many times for our Egypt and Jordan trips, who was well acquainted with Pakistan as well. He was liaising with a local Pakistani travel agent. As usual, Richard Searight and I were responsible for the Brooke side and for the general welfare of the supporters.

Our hotel in Lahore was splendid! Shining marble, sparkling chandeliers, greetings with cool, fruity drinks after our long haul. Spacious rooms, clean sheets and breakfast to die for. So we all found it extremely discomforting to return each afternoon to our western-style palace after a day in the field. In fact, this has always been a fundamental problem with supporter tours: how to reconcile the experiences of the day with our relatively luxurious return in the evening. But isn't this a conundrum of life? I think about it often at home, as I lie back on my comfortable mattress at the end of a well-furnished day, with a heart full of gratitude for my lot. Brigadier Hassan Sami once explained to me, when I wondered at the equanimity, grace, dignity and total life-acceptance of the rubbish collectors in the Mokattam Hills of Cairo, that, according to local religious belief, everyone is given a cup of a certain size and it is therefore pointless to question what is given. One's cup is always full. Knowing that one's cup is always full can only lead to one place – acceptance of what is.

So what are we, the Brooke, doing in Pakistan, or anywhere else, for that matter? Why are we bothering? Well, for the sake of the suffering animals, of course. And because, for the people, hand in hand with acceptance can walk suffering. And there are those people, such as Dorothy Brooke, with enough sensibility to notice. Although this might sound a rather sweeping statement, I do believe that humanity is divided into two: the givers and the takers. That is not such a simple division as it first appears. Unconditional givers want to share, no matter how little they already have. I remember being so moved at that Indian brick kiln when I was plied with hot chai served from a bucket - and biscuits as well! This was such an honour and such generosity. Daring, then, to take a further step into this apparently black and white comparison, there are two types of takers: those who take with gratitude, without wishing to stop the cyclic flow of giving and receiving, and those who take with fear, so that the flow stops and stagnates. Of course, we are all givers and takers, and we all simply take turn to be either. It's the taking turn which counts. And at every giving and taking shift, there is a little, sometimes imperceptible, rise in our quality of life at that moment, even in our quality of heart. Some moments might be brief; others might be life-changing, particularly if the Brooke is included in the cycle. In general, givers (which undoubtedly make up the body of Brooke Hospital supporters) also possess a great quality which I feel is the balm which anoints all the bruises of life: compassion.

Each morning, we left the hotel, bags packed to the hilt with water, sunscreen, cameras and left-over breakfast for the feral dogs and cats (this latter became a cause for some disharmony if we gave good food to the dogs in front of local people and we had to cease this little ritual). But by far the lightest and most universally held item in the bag was compassion, mixed with a genuine interest and desire to meet people from another land with respect and love. I'm sure our supporters would not see themselves in these terms, but that is exactly what I witnessed each day. So much love. Can you love people you don't know and will never see again? Can you love animals you meet only fleetingly? Of course, when there is love already residing in a person's heart, it doesn't differentiate. It just spills out to wherever and whatever happens to turn up. If there is an abiding experience of all my trips with supporters overseas, this is it. And that we could return to a hot shower after a day of sharing such a commodity on the streets and in the brick kilns? Well, perhaps the only thing left for us is to be grateful, not uncomfortable. The size of our cup then happened to include a hot shower, if not a private plane or merely a one-roomed shack. It's just the way things work out.

Compassion in action

I have just led you up a philosophical garden path, a digression which, for me, is probably one of the greatest understandings arising from my entire time with the Brooke.

The hotel also redeemed its luxurious self. It wrote notices for us addressed to the honoured guests of the honoured Brooke Hospital for Animals. And we were honoured with the most magnificent horse's head, life-size, carved in ice! We were absolutely freezing, since they had turned up the air-conditioning in the room, to keep it from melting. We might have savoured even more gratefully the luxury of that hotel, had we known what some of the others would be like later in the trip!

The trip was arduous. Seeing the work was always a total experience – exhilarating, exhausting, emotional. Our first experience of the work was at the Shalimar Gardens where the Brooke van had stopped under a raised canopy. The animals were in very poor condition. The team was

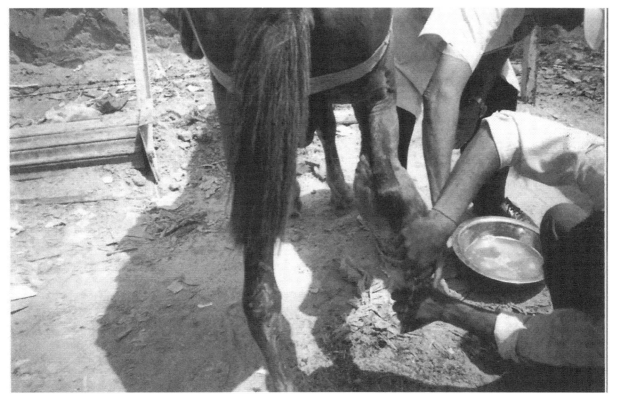

Very lame animal

very efficient and everyone was orderly and quiet. This was a general experience throughout Pakistan. We had not been operating there very long, just a couple of years, and most of the animals we saw were in very poor condition. However, their owners were very enthusiastic about the presence of the Brooke vets and seemed ready to listen to advice. Years down the line, of course, our methods have been refined and refined again, and we are making huge inroads.

But then, all I can say is that we saw some heart-breaking sights. Our Brooke itinerary would take us to clinics in Peshawar, Multan, Shalimar, Charsadda Road and Gujranwala.

As I have said, seeing the work at any time is always a heart-rending and heart-uplifting experience. During those early trips, when the Brooke hadn't been going that long in Pakistan or India, we saw so many poor, thin animals. But we were all so impressed by the vets, who all spoke excellent English and whose manner was, without exception, confident and commanding in the field.

Pakistani brick kiln

Yet, when we spoke to them, they were modest about their skills and understanding of the owners' problems. They really had compassion themselves and always continued to work until the last animal had been seen, regardless of the length of their working day. I remarked to them that this showed great dedication. The reply came back that they were dedicated both to their animals and to their profession. It was said very simply and I knew it was true. At that time, they were already talking about wishing to discuss problems with other Brooke vets in other

Brooke farrier at work

parts of the world. Now, thanks to the great god, Computer, this can happen with ease as they share things in virtual discussions and circulating reports on line. They also meet up each year physically.

It is so vital that the Brooke approach, the Brooke methodology, the Brooke standard are all consistently adhered to throughout the world and this can only happen through communication. In the days of those early tours we made, we hadn't reached that refinement in our management of communication. However, the individual vets' own professional ethic was enough to keep us going on the right track, coupled with excellent management from the top. I was told by one of the vets that the owners trusted them so completely that they would travel 50 miles to have their horse treated by the vet they knew, if he had happened to transfer to another team. The head vet at the time was Anwar ul Haq. The staff spoke very warmly of him and said he "inspired unity and effort". They told me that it was because of him that everything was so well ordered. My Brooke room-mate on that trip, Vivienne, said she was sorry she would never see Anwar ul Haq again - "the sort of person you never want to let out of your life." She said it with great emotion and respect.

In Pakistan, supporter trips were always busy with social events, as each of the Pakistani trustees wanted to share their hospitality. They were all wealthy men and their homes reflected this. Their large houses were filled with treasures, so that I would almost feel I needed that National Trust card once more to gain entry; always someone at hand to serve you with drinks and food. I remember one dinner where the entire group was seated round an enormous dining table overseen personally by our host and hostess, who were so kind and welcoming. We seemed to be surrounded by Ming vases! I was interested to learn how much charitable work the wives of our trustees did, particularly for women. They were highly intelligent women with horizons that went far wider than their palatial homes.

Colonel Moheen, one of our senior staff in Lahore, was someone I could have taken home in my pocket. And he went through every difficulty like a hot knife through butter. If there was a problem, Colonel Moheen would sort it out. He was the solution, just by being Colonel Moheen.

When we visited the daily "dance" that took place on the border between the Indian and Pakistan Armies at dawn and dusk – the raising and lowering of their respective flags (more on that later) – Colonel Moheen led us through every checkpoint just by saying his name. Guards bowed their

Multan clinic

heads like reeds in the wind. And yet, with all his air of quiet authority, he was so gentle, kind and respectful. On a visit to the Shalimar Gardens in Lahore, our party was enjoying a tea laid on especially for us under an ornate shelter overlooking the fountains. A young ragamuffin started to hang around the group. I saw Moheen go up to him, place a fatherly arm round his shoulder, and lead him away, explaining (I discovered afterwards) who we were and that his presence wasn't appropriate. There was no scolding or belittling. His manner brought tears to the eyes of this observer.

There was a similar incident once, when I was in Pakistan on a later visit. John Trampleasure and I were accompanying a team which had stopped at its regular road-side station. We were being just a little bit bothered by a man who was begging. The vet in charge went up to him, put an arm around his shoulder, and gently led him away, explaining who we were and what it was all about. It was all done with the utmost respect and compassion. He was talking to the man as an equal. Again, I was moved to tears.

A very frail donkey enjoying his last meal

This gentleness and respect was always shown to the animals, too. A mental image that will forever be with me is that of a particularly frail-looking little donkey at Multan Clinic. His owner had bought him six months earlier, very cheaply because of his condition, and had hoped that he would improve. Looking at his malnourished and unkempt condition, I didn't believe that its current owner had done much to contribute to the poor creature's welfare. But at least he had brought it to the Brooke for us to work a miracle. The donkey's tears, caused by an eye infection – which the Brooke vet treated immediately – and his withered, weathered and weary frame were so poignant that I wept myself. He was immediately deemed a humane destruction case and later on I was relieved to see him at the clinic, contently showing just a few more signs of life as he munched his way through gourmet green fodder, tail swishing. An assistant was gently brushing away the mud and filth coating his matted mane. He was due to go in a day or so but he was lovingly being smartened up, prepared for a dignified end. Mrs Brooke would have been proud to see her own compassion mirrored so perfectly.

As part of our sightseeing in Pakistan, we were taken to see two very different-looking mosques; one, in Lahore, was built in the traditional style and it was interesting to see how groups of attentive men would gather around the Imam to listen to him expound on the Koran. The atmosphere was quiet and studious. In contrast, we visited a mosque in Islamabad, this time very modern in its architecture. Islamabad is a very new, angular and rather boring looking city, built in blocks alongside the softer, more colonial atmosphere of Rawalpindi. I didn't have any headgear and decided to sit on the grass outside. I attracted some attention: a Western woman sitting cross-legged on the ground on her own! Soon a family had gathered around me and we started to communicate. "Talk" would not have been an appropriate word to use. But it was amazing how we did manage to communicate. When our guide came to "rescue" me, we really got going with his help. Afterwards two of the children presented me with roses!

Another abiding memory of our visit to Lahore which, by the way, is known as the garden city of Pakistan, is a visit to the tomb of its most famous Poet Laureate, Jullaudhari. This was a special mission entrusted to me by my Pakistani friend, Zia, who is his daughter. His tomb was swathed in a green cloth covered with fresh flowers. In the atmosphere of love and reverence which abided, I bowed and asked for blessings for his soul and also for his daughter.

Reclining woman, Taxila Museum

After Lahore and its amazing contrasts of wealth and poverty that we saw in the Brooke's field of work, we were to start an exciting part of the trip: driving along the Karakoram Highway, one of the old silk routes, as far as the Chinese border. We started out from Rawalpindi. There were twenty-one of us and we were divided into two small minibuses, since the roads we were about to meet were not suited to larger vehicles. We took a route via the ancient site of Taxila, a Buddhist city. I still have on my kitchen wall a postcard depicting one of the statues in the museum. It shows a reclining woman and you can hardly believe that she isn't about to get up for a stretch, so lifelike is she. We wandered around the low-lying walls that marked the extent of habitation. One enduring memory I have is of a couple on the trip who were fond of walking.

They were both extraordinarily tall and their long legs carried them way into the distance. I thought we'd never see them again.

As this particular couple has come to mind, one of the best birthdays I have ever had was shared with the husband on this trip. We shared a huge cake and delicious supper seated at tables round a swimming pool.

Negotiating a waterfall en route

We continued on our way towards our lunchtime watering stop. It had been a long and picturesque drive, and now we were climbing higher and higher through darker and darker pine forests. We arrived late at our stop and the clouds were closing in. We resumed our journey in pouring rain and I could see that our guide, Anwar, was getting concerned. We were aiming for a small town called Besham where we had been booked in at the local government-run hostel. The rain became quite heavy and the road was getting narrower.

At one point, it disappeared completely, washed away by a heavy waterfall. We had no option but to pass under the waterfall! Amazing! As we climbed higher, we could see the river valley below, far below. Sometimes, the minibus would be just inches away from the edge. The

View on the Karakoram Highway, Hindu Khush

bridges appeared very rickety and twice we all had to disembark. The bridge could not have taken the weight of the vehicle and its passengers together. The roads were so treacherous that they were closed soon after we had passed through, but I can't say I felt any real fear. The drivers were totally in control and knew the route by the inch. They proved this by saying, at one time, that we would soon come to some rocks carved with ancient writings. And an hour later, we did! Thank goodness, we eventually arrived safely at our destination and our sleeping quarters.

The Karakoram Highway offered us such diverse scenery. At first, the river was far below, looking heavy, like molten lead, with islands of logs being floated along. That was a sad sight. The loss of forest on a vast scale is the reason for the huge loss of agricultural topsoil resulting in great hardship for farmers. It is also the main cause of more and more frequent disastrous flooding. But the scenery we were passing through then was breathtakingly beautiful. I remember one part where I so wished I were a painter.

I'll try with words.

The river was flowing along a deep but wide gorge, the sides of which rippled in huge, curtain-like formations, rather like the curved buttresses of a castle. At the top, the gently rising land was green with rice fields, the white horizontals of its stone terracing forming a contrast with the verticals of feathery poplar trees, just coming into spring leaf. Dotted about in the distance were clumps of pink or white cotton-wool trees – apricot blossom in full bloom. Further into the distance, as the terraced fields climbed the foothills, one could just about discern a few small villages of flat-roofed houses nestling discreetly in the shelter of the hills, hardly making a mark of human habitation on the scene. And the hills then rolled away higher, ever higher, towards peak upon snow-capped peak of magnificent mountains, all against a backdrop of an increasingly pink and golden sunset sky. It was breath-taking. Eventually we would climb high enough to see the peak of K2 glistening in the evening rose-light.

Meantime, we had to stop en route, either for a picnic lunch, or to wait for the Army to come and remove a landslide which was blocking our path. One of our party decided to sit on a rock to eat her lunch. The next moment, I saw Anwar make a cricketer's dive for her as the rock started to slide down the hillside, taking its occupant with it!

The glacier's end!

I have walked on a glacier! I can't say that I was very impressed. It appeared to be a dirty stream of rocks and debris making imperceptibly slow progress down a hillside and across the road. I was in short sleeves and it was hot! But I was assured it was a glacier. On another occasion, we all got out to look for garnets. They were strewn all over the road and I have a handful now, still waiting to be polished. Does anyone reading this have the means?!

Gilgit, our next stop, is a gateway town to more remote areas and we had to pass through it to reach the Hunza Valley and beyond. It is famous for its polo and we attended a match. We had seen many horses en route, being ridden up to the town in readiness for the match. This is a pretty high elevation and the horses were being asked to perform at low oxygen levels after having walked long distances. So, you can understand that our attendance was controversial to

Young beauties of Karimabad

some of our party. But those who went enjoyed the excitement and skill displayed. Gilgit also has a wonderful bazaar – my undoing was the fabric shops. They were piled high with bales of beautiful fine cotton and amazing silk, most of it from China. I still have some of that silk, waiting to be transformed into underwear, outerwear and all the other dreams that stuff is made of…..

Man ploughing with yak, Nultur Valley

As we climbed yet higher, the river changed its nature. We had already passed the confluence of three great rivers – the Ganges, the Naltur and the Hunza - and were making our way up the Hunza Valley. The air was becoming quite thin and one or two were suffering from altitude sickness. I seemed to have a touch of flu.

In fact, one lady was so affected by altitude sickness that she was eventually wheel-chaired to our plane at the departure airport. But we had arrived at Karimabad, which seemed to be on the top of the world. It was the most wonderful little town. In none of the towns had we seen a woman on the street and this was no exception. However, there seemed to be a festival of some sort going on in the town centre and some women were about, but, at our touristy appearance, they fled into the background once more.

Many of the people here are red-haired and pale-skinned, perhaps a heritage of the Alexandrine era. They live to a ripe old age in the Hunza Valley. I'm not surprised. Their diet is very healthy, though rather heavy on apricots. We had apricot soup, apricot stew, apricot sauce, apricot pie and dried apricots to nibble as snacks.

The air is unpolluted and the stress of the London Stock Exchange certainly passes them all by. People work well into their centenary years. On a jeep excursion, we passed one very elderly man ploughing his field with his yak. It was a small field and when we returned an hour and a half later he had almost finished.

Truck decorated in traditional fashion

We had hoped to reach China but that experience was not to be.

A rather more serious landslide had blocked the road further along and it would take the Army some days to clear it. So, about 60 kilometres from our goal, we were forced to turn back.

We were an interesting bunch on that trip, ranging from a couple who had dedicated their lives to and spent their entire income on hands-on animal welfare (they eventually moved to India to continue this) to a couple who owned a lucrative veal-producing farm. Both couples were lovely

and ardent, generous supporters of the Brooke's work. However, there were moments when my skills in diplomacy were tested to the limit. In between these extremes we encompassed a journalist passionate about animal welfare and various other dedicated animal and horse lovers, including our wonderfully forgetful Brooke supporter and her brother, who was there to keep her out of trouble (yes, the same pair!). One night, I shared a room with said lady, who was trying to escape her snoring brother. She put up some stiff competition herself, I have to say…

There is often one person on a trip with the potential to be a bit tricky. This trip was blessed with two - a married couple. I noticed how they were always first up and breakfasted in order to make sure they had the front seat by the driver – the best view. They came to consider it as their seat. One morning, I was amused to see that everyone had got up extremely early, before this couple, and someone else had snaffled the front seat!

Returning to Peshawar from such dizzy heights could have been an anti-climax but our route took us through the Swat Valley. We have heard it mentioned quite a lot in the news lately. The Taliban were not influential in the area

Quiet corner, Peshawar Clinic

when we visited it and it was then a peaceful, beautiful part of the world. We stayed in a relic of the colonial era – an amazing hotel built round a charming quadrangle. It was all marble and gilt. As usual, I was sharing a room with Vivienne. Our bathroom was enormous. We switched on the light. The bedding was unkempt, the bath was unkempt, the room was unkempt and ....we had everything made kempt before we would touch it. English kempt and Pakistani kempt don't always tally.

We finally arrived in Peshawar and pollution. I remember how I felt in Karimabad. Life could be so simple. I could live there for six months of the year and back in London for six months.

Peshawar Clinic entrance

Actually, I just didn't want to leave the place. Peshawar was the antidote to all that. Dusty, bustling, noisy. The animals all seemed to be in an appalling condition – which was why Brooke was there, of course. We stayed in the famous Dean's Hotel. I can't think why it was famous. It stank of dank. Colonel Khush had invited us to his club, the Peshawar Club, for dinner. This was the oldest club in Pakistan, being founded in 1846, and Khush had been a member since 1947!

The next day was a Brooke field day and we saw the clinic. It emanated a very peaceful and inviting air, with its grassy paddocks and bougainvillea climbing up the walls. The animals everywhere looked totally emaciated and in a debilitated condition. I'd like to go back now, just to see for myself the difference I know we have made in the intervening years.

We were also taken to the vast Pajaggi Fair, where animals are bought and sold. That day it was particularly busy, as animals were being traded for the Eid slaughter. The horses were very poor and one old chestnut with ossified knees caught my attention. Actually, it caught my heart and made me cry. This apparently moved the owner sufficiently for him to agree to sell his horse for humane destruction. After a little bargaining, our man bought it for R600. I thanked the man for agreeing to the sale and we shook hands. He followed us to the exit and thanked me again. At that time, Pajaggi Fair was new on our list and I felt quite helpless about the size of the task ahead. How could we measure up to the desperate need which was so obvious?

Pajaggi Fair

I have brought this first trip to Pakistan to the table in greater detail, perhaps because it is still so vivid in my mind, even all these years later. I have hardly had to refer to my notebook, except to remember place names.

I am sure the same goes for all the participants, though, very sadly, two of them, my room companion and my birthday companion, have since passed away.

I found these lines at the back of my journal:

The Nultar Valley
Silver-grey lace veiled the mountainside.
Soft, ethereal, the bushes floated on the slopes.

Pakistani spectators and soldiers at Wagha

I can't leave this amazing country without sharing just a couple, or three, more of my most vivid Brooke moments.

One memorable Brooke "moment" encountered during my trip to Pakistan was that daily ceremonial dance between the Pakistan and Indian armies which I mentioned earlier. This takes place at Wagha, a location at the border between the two countries. At sunrise, the Indian and Pakistani flags are raised. And sunset is the time when local people and visitors from far and wide go to watch the lowering of the flags, thousands of them on both sides of the border.

We drove from Lahore and joined the queue of vehicles forming along the approach road. This was where Colonel Moheen's name cut through the butter. Space was made for us to drive straight through. We were escorted through the throng of spectators along to our allotted privileged front-row seating to watch the spectacle that would unfold. There were stands of tiered seats on both sides of the marching area where the spectators were already chanting "Pakistan! Pakistan!" as they tried to outdo the vocals going on further down on the other side of the strip of "no-man's land" dividing the two territories. The other side was chanting "Hindustan! Hindustan!" The respective flags were being slowly lowered as the sun finally set, amidst great trumpet fanfares and cheers and catcalls and more football arena type chanting from the stands to support each "team".

However, the most exciting part of the ceremony was what preceded this final ritual of lowering the flags: a lengthy and distinctly acrobatic yet, at the same time, ceremonial marching and displaying of arms. And legs! Nazi frog-marching had nothing on this. The soldiers had to march while lifting their legs like the Tiller Girls. (Who remembers them?!) Each soldier had obviously been picked for his height and length of leg, which was exaggerated by stacked shoes and outrageously tall headgear.

They all sported belligerent, extravagant, black and glossy moustaches. (Dad, eat your heart out!) One man lifted his leg just a jot too sharpish and banged his own nose quite violently. We were falling off our seats with laughter. The whole event was quite bizarre, demonstrating how amazingly funny all our human antics must look from Heaven's viewpoint! Heaven itself was indeed an incredible backdrop of blood-red streaks striating a pale azure sky. Its dramatic colours matched the high drama and tension of the pantomime below.

And it didn't finish there. Afterwards, we were all shepherded to a special area where we were then served with tea and delicacies, followed by a slow roam in the Pakistan gloaming round the quiet fields which bounded the site. It was all quite unforgettable. [If you want to see it all for yourself, you can do so by searching on the web with a group of key words such as *Pakistan, India, border, flag ceremony*.]

And then.... Up The Khyber Pass! We were most fortunate to be one of the last parties of tourists to be taken by steam train up the Khyber Pass before security issues prevented further journeys.

The Khyber Pass steam locomotive

A very enterprising Pakistani businessman had restored the locomotive and carriages, as well as the track, which had originally been expertly laid by British Army engineers in the previous century. We, too, were back in another era. How incongruous looked our jeans and sneakers, our sunglasses and backpacks! Well, of course, I am from another era, so I wasn't wearing jeans and sneakers, or a backpack. But even this old relic from the past was not prepared for the amazing reception we received at every station en route.

Our first stop up the Khyber

We were advised not to worry too much if we happened to notice a man with a rifle crouching on a rock at various intervals along the line. This should not be taken personally. He was probably just guarding his own property. Well, some of those properties were definitely worth guarding - enormous and hidden behind high walls. One could just make out the tops of trees and a glint of water shining in the sun. Swimming pool, perhaps? Poppies, ah, poppies….you are so beautiful, so versatile. …

Our party sat in high-backed seats as in an old railway carriage. The rest of the carriage was taken up with Japanese tourists. It was all very reminiscent of Agatha Christie and I wondered which of us would go first. I suddenly felt the need for Hercule Poirot…

We proceeded out of the terminus amid much cheering and steaming and whistle-blowing to our first stop. As we went on our way, people came out of their houses to wave, children scrambled up trees and rocks to whistle and call and, yes, I did see a few gents on rocks, but no artillery in sight. We passed low mud dwellings behind high walls, with gun towers in their courtyards, as well as some rather well-appointed large houses with beautiful gardens, telephone wires and TV aerials and the occasional flash of swimming pool blue.

View from the carriage

The group with Afghanistan as our backdrop

As we approached the first station, I was intrigued to hear the faint sounds of a very British-sounding brass band. Slowly puffing to a halt, with the whistle blowing at full blast, we saw a sight we thought we would never see anywhere outside the British Isles – a military band, complete with bagpipes, parading in kilts and berets and full paraphernalia to the sound of a very English tune, the kind that gets the troops marching.

And heading them all up was their mace bearer and their mascot – a beautiful ram with plaid decorations! We were all expected to disembark and thank them, which we did, of course. It had been staged for us and us alone! And then we were on our way again.

Some chose to go to the front of the train, face the wind and steam and be intrepid. As we made very slow progress higher up the pass, there were times when the track performed a hairpin bend.

The old engineering was so ingenious. The carriages were unhooked from the engine, which had halted on a turntable on which it was rotated until it was facing the right direction to go up the next bit of track. Of course the carriages were still facing the wrong way when they were eventually reunited with the engine. But those canny engineers had thought of that, too. We were all asked to stand up while our seats backs were swung to slope in the opposite direction. Simple! We sat down, completely, simply and successfully re-orientated.

The terrain was just as Colonel Khush, Colonel Thompson and John Brocklehurst would have encountered: rocky, barren, dry and very uninviting. We chuffed along slowly, stopping at another station where we were treated to an enormous "mid-morning snack" of tea, sandwiches and cakes inside the station house (which no-one really wanted, knowing that there would be a good lunch further up), until we reached the Officers' Mess situated at the end of the line, at a part of the pass which overlooks Afghanistan. We were looking at Afghanistan! Lunch was sumptuous, served with army formality, though the sandwiches had rather spoiled my appetite for it. And even more dancing to celebrate our arrival. What an experience!

My last visit to Pakistan was in the company of my boss, John Trampleasure, then our Director of Fundraising. He hadn't seen the work in that country and I hadn't been for some years, so it was decided – we would go together. The experience was quite different this time. Apart from the fact that I didn't have a party of supporters to look after and could really concentrate on the work, it was the work itself that had developed by leaps and bounds. The condition of the animals, too, had improved enormously wherever the Brooke was working. There was much more a sense of going out to meet the owners where they were at, rather than hoping or even expecting them to meet the staff where they were. So the teams would be willing to work different hours, to go to the animals' places of rest, to travel with an owner on his cart in order to find out the causes of his animal's problems. There was a much closer relationship with the people, trying to see their working day from their point of view and fitting in with that. Work in the brick kilns included simply monitoring the activities of the animals and making recommendations based on observation.

Donkey owner, kiln owner and other workers with Brooke's Dr Shahabat

The brick kilns are always the final straw for me. Hell on Earth. However, we were taken to one brick kiln and I honestly thought, "This is Heaven!" Heaven for me is where everything works smoothly and to everyone's equal benefit. As we approached this particular kiln, I noticed that there were trees around and inside the perimeter walls. A couple of men were quietly seated in the shade, talking. We were taken through the gate and met by a man with a very good face – keen eyes which looked straight at you. He was the owner of all the animals that worked the kiln. He rented them out. He was the builder of this Heaven. Before the Brooke came, he was desperate. His animals were dying. One day he went to the owner of the brick kiln with fifteen donkeys' tails in his hand. He said he couldn't afford to continue and asked the owner to bring in the Brooke for their advice and support. The owner agreed, fortunately. So the Brooke came and immediately arranged for a bore well to be sunk, with the help of another charitable agency, which provided the pump. Fresh water was then available for the first time for an area of two or three square kilometres. Imagine the impact on the local people. The owner agreed to supply bricks to build a shade shelter and the workers provided the labour.

On the day we arrived, the shade shelter had been decorated with a huge WELCOME! And, believe it or not, there was a ribbon across its length, waiting to be ceremoniously cut! I was asked to do the honours. I wonder whether the Queen has ever felt the emotions that were running through me as I cut that ribbon. It was a remarkable Brooke moment. There were already animals using the shelter and they all looked in very good condition indeed. The owner of the kiln had provided tea and refreshments for us and we were so moved by their hospitality. He told us that he always made a point of coming to the Brooke training sessions which happened every Friday after prayers. Such an interest in the day-to-day running of his kiln is rare in an owner.

The animal owner had tried to influence a neighbouring kiln but to no avail. So he bought the suffering animals from that kiln and had them recuperate under the care of the Brooke and pure running water. Now, our staff tells us that there is a waiting list of kilns, asking the Brooke to work with them. Isn't that heavenly news for a Brooke supporter?

Fresh drinking water at last!

Egypt – Again!

I want to return to Egypt at the end of this chapter since the last trip I organised for Brooke supporters took place in Egypt in 2009. This was a special trip to mark our 75th anniversary and to celebrate the Brooke's achievements in the country of its founding. Another key objective of this particular trip was to generate awareness of the Brooke's work across the UK media. The more coverage, the more people will engage and understand how important our work is. We had a wonderful collection of people, some of whom were seasoned Brooke trippers.

Before we all get to the airport, I can tell you that a lot of work has taken place. In fact, eighteen months' worth. It takes that long to organise a Brooke supporters' trip overseas. Apart from advertising the trip in due time for people to plan ahead, the main problem then to overcome is communicating exactly what you want to happen day by day, hour by hour, to the travel agent – who knows very well how to organise tourists to see the sights but nothing about the vagaries of working with a team of vets   – and also to the overseas staff – who want to show off the work but have no idea of the problems of moving 30 people around it, as well as incorporating the tourist bits. There is always competition for the time available to do both to everyone's complete satisfaction. Communicating words is relatively easy. But communicating ideas, communicating opportunities, communicating possible pitfalls is an art in itself. Spreadsheets are the answer! We created one spreadsheet after another, with colours and codes and columns. And timing is everything! No-one but me seemed to understand this. If the travel agent said it would take an hour to get from A to B, who was I to argue with him? But I always did! I knew that in Egypt it never took an hour. It always took at least two hours. And that was just the journey time. First of all, you had to gather the troops. So I always allowed plenty of room for manoeuvre. And, boy, did we need it! A little tip: when you want to gather your troops, always ask them to arrive fifteen minutes before the time you want them to arrive. This can be a problem for those who like to be early and are then forced to wait half an hour. So tell them the truth and they are soon on side.

We wanted to include Alexandria this time and that did complicate things. We also wanted to end up in Cairo for a grand finale. So we started with a Nile trip, flying to Luxor and taking the cruiser to Aswan, visiting Edfu en route.

Luxor

"Ah!"

It was wonderful to be back in Luxor again, though very different from the previous visits. The Brooke was now in its later premises, having made the move in late 2005 from its delightful little clinic near the centre of the town because of the archaeological works near the site, to a larger space further out of town at Naga el Khataba. This was the new hub from which radiated the vet teams. They could go further afield and found that their reach expanded enormously. At the time of our visit the teams served 23 communities in the town and surrounding villages and also spent a lot of time training and working with local organisations, particularly those which facilitated communication with women.

However, it was marvellous to see how owners were bringing in their animals into the clinic, too, for a refreshing wash down or a good roll in the sandpits. This also gave the staff an opportunity to look over the animals. I noticed that the owners were much more hands-on with their animals within the clinic confines, not leaving everything to the staff. Great stuff! One of the best moments for me was being greeted on our arrival by the staff, many of whom had been

Dr Amin in teaching mode

with the Brooke since Luxor had opened all those years ago. It felt like family and I felt like a close family member. Tears.......!

To see the work in the field our party divided into smaller groups. I was in a group conducted by Dr Amin to the west bank of the River Nile outside a stable housing some camels. It was so airy and shady and as peaceful as a church! A Luxor Clinic mobile team has been visiting the west bank since the new bridge across the Nile was built in 1998 and the team manages to reach almost all the 2,800 equine animals working there in various capacities.

There was a light-bulb moment for me while talking to the vet on the way to the location; Dr Amin told me how their work was having such an impact on the welfare and condition of the donkeys, after ten years of hard labour on his patch, that the purchase price of donkeys had actually risen.

Whereas previously a donkey had been at the bottom of the league, it was now expensive enough for an owner to value it more highly, and that included its welfare. He told me that it had been the custom for owners to let animals suffer until the Brooke vets came by on their regular visits. But those higher purchase prices had changed attitudes sufficiently to force owners to look for treatment in between Brooke visits. Having to pay for treatment not only encouraged the owner to be more careful with his animal but also supported local vets and pharmacies. The Brooke was still supporting the whole process by being on the end of a phone, advising the owner where to go. This led to local practitioners viewing the Brooke not as competition but as an ally and source of knowledge. Such a change in emphasis by the Brooke has brought about monumental change in its relationships with owners, local practitioners, pharmacies and NGOs and I was bowled over by all the positive ramifications of this policy. I then saw how it was being practised wherever we went, making owners more responsible and local veterinary services more consultative and willing to be trained by Brooke. It was a win-win situation which could only lead to a sustainable and expanding future for our work and I felt so excited by it all. But it was still a tough call trying to change the mindset of some owners. Old habits die hard.

Early morning serenity

Probably the most relaxing time of the whole trip was sailing up the Nile on a luxurious cruise boat. We planned this to give our travellers some respite from the rigours of the day. Those unforgettable early mornings on deck watching the sun rise as we floated past quiet villages with their thatched houses, and the long dark line of hills marking the edge of agrarian terrain. Small boats would just be starting out on their business, the river lapping and the serene water gleaming in the early morning light. Heaven!

The evenings were wonderful, too. Cooler, calmer. Except for the night of the party, of course. We were all asked to dress for the occasion. That meant purchasing outfits that would shimmer and shake and dazzle and dare! Yes, we were all invited to dance Egyptian style. Some memorable moments were to be shared as we wibbled and wobbled our way around the floor to the engaging rhythm of the music. Even I let my hair down. Well, the phrase doesn't quite suit my crowning glory, but you know what I mean.

Every evening of the trip, I called a meeting. It was essential that we had watertight timings and that everything went like clockwork, otherwise arrangements fell apart. We reviewed our plans and, despite all the earlier planning by spreadsheet, lots had to be changed as local circumstances demanded. Trying to find a balance between seeing the sights and seeing the work was impossible since each participant had different aspirations for the trip. Some were only interested in Brooke and others, having been invited as a partner or to keep the supporter company, put Brooke's work much further down their list of priorities, though one lady who knew nothing about the work, and had no intention whatsoever of seeing it, was totally converted to the role of fundraiser after reluctantly having had to join a Brooke visit.

Meantime, I felt like an army general and was probably looked on as behaving like one. But I had no choice. And sometimes it fell apart anyway! How can one plan for the lady whom we lost in the Temple of Horus? She had wandered away from her companion who looked everywhere, while I looked everywhere else. Not a sighting. We were now greatly delayed. It then occurred to me that she might have returned to our coach. And there she was, asking why had we taken so long to return and where were we having tea and where was her walking stick...?

Edfu

Edfu Clinic was a revelation! Although we had had high hopes for this beautifully designed oasis when it opened in 1992, it had been a very tough job to change the attitude of local people, not just the animal owners but the other townsfolk, too. How many times had Brooke tried to establish water troughs and shade shelters, only to have them removed by locals who didn't want the animals near their backyard. Now that had all changed. We were delighted to see a beautiful shade shelter outside the Temple of Horus and the clinic was actively encouraging the installation of more shelters and water troughs in the vicinity.

Shade shelter outside Temple of Horus, Edfu

Edfu clinic had expanded to 31 boxes, their worming programme covered well over 21,000 animals in a year and the projects they were engaged in included training local animal health providers, school visits, working with the Women's Associations Federation and local government. Importantly, the clinic had appointed female Rural Guides to help each team disseminate animal welfare messages, collect data, and advise where new animal needs were greatest. When we visited the clinic, a training session was in full swing on harness-making using soft woven cotton webbing. This was a real Brooke moment for me. After seeing all our literature spread around the coffee shop at the Temple of Horus, I couldn't have been more impressed with all the initiatives that Edfu clinic was adopting.

Aswan

Aswan has been operating since 1988. I loved its air of quiet efficiency and its story has been one of expansion over the years, with teams reaching 32 locations and more than 24,000 animals. We were all rather shocked by two very bad cases brought into the clinic during our brief visit: a very lame donkey and a traffic accident case.

Feeding station, Aswan Clinic

Alexandria

Alexandria is one of my favourite cities. There is an air of dilapidated charm about this very European place. Its buildings and wide boulevards are redolent with faded Mediterranean glory. We had driven by coach from Cairo. This is not the most enjoyable of journeys – heavy traffic, desert all the way - it just seems interminable. I decided to relieve the boredom by talking to my captive audience about the work and our change of emphasis. I remember feeling my own enthusiasm for the direction the Brooke was taking towards even further empowering the animal owners by making sure they took more responsibility for the welfare of their animals. I shared with everyone in the coach my lightbulb moment with Dr Amin. In addition, the Brooke was making far greater use of existing organisations to reach out to people: for example, the Rural Guides who were being trained by us to take their knowledge to their own communities. There were many examples of such lateral thinking in Brooke Egypt's current work. The talk transformed a boring journey into a more informative one.

When we finally arrived in Alexandria, we sat and ate our packed lunch with a view of the sea, the sun warming our backs and good-natured stall-holders vying for our attention. We had some packed lunches left over so I offered them to the men, who seemed delighted and offered me a necklace as a gift - an exchange of goodwill which even now, as I write about it, brings a warm glow.

Goodwill can sometimes be misplaced, however. During one of our field excursions – to Kafra ad Dawwar about 45 minutes from Alex – some of our group started to proffer apples previously gleaned from the breakfast buffet, but the vet on duty, Dr Mohamed, immediately asked them to refrain. He explained that when the animal owners couldn't afford to buy apples for their own children, it was hard for them to watch us feeding good apples to their horses. Life is so subtle, is it not? There is such a fine line we have to tread, especially between cultures, between social groups. Although it is great to act from the heart, a bit of head has to be involved to ensure there is no misunderstanding, no hurt, no grounds for envy or perception of difference. I was reminded of our experiences in Pakistan when supporters packed their bags and pockets with breakfast left-overs to feed to stray dogs and cats, only to be told to refrain for the same reasons.

We enjoyed watching the vet at work as the owners/users queued with their animals for treatment while local community members kept order. At one point one of the owners was chastised by a local community member for tying his horse too tightly to a tree and, insulted, the man was about to walk away. A Brooke supporter, realising that the man's horse actually looked in very good condition, managed to persuade the owner to stay for treatment. I think the vet and the community members who witnessed the incident were impressed with this little intercession by a "layman".

After an enjoyable and enlightening visit to the Brooke work in Alex, plus its tourist attractions, we were faced with the long drive back to Cairo. Undaunted, I decided to relieve the boredom yet again with a talk to my captive audience, this time about money. I decided that these supporters, who had given so much, seen so much and now understood so much, still had no idea what went on behind the scenes to facilitate all that they had seen – and how much such facilitation cost. I spent a very useful hour telling them about every aspect of the London office's work, everyone's role in the great play, how the jigsaw fitted together and what it cost.

Cairo

Cairo was where it had all begun. I could sense the pride in the welcome we were given on arrival at the Hospital and in the way we were conducted during our tour round the several buildings which now comprise it. The spacious sandy recuperation areas were as tranquil as ever, with animals enjoying good food and shade – and like-minded company! Inside, almost all the boxes were full –all traffic accidents.

We were organised into smaller groups, as usual, so that our numbers overwhelmed neither the animals, their owners nor our patient Brooke vets. I shall describe my own particular group's field visit to the brick kilns of Helwan later.

Apart from seeing the work in the field, Brooke supporters also wanted to avail themselves of as much of Cairo's rich plate as possible. And I wanted to give everyone as much opportunity within the time available. This meant that my planning skills were put to the test. But how can one plan for getting lost en route to an Arab stud farm on the outskirts of Cairo? We had a complicated day ahead with multiple sightseeing choices for our travellers. Won't do that again…. Disaster! The options were seeing some wonderful tapestry work at the Wassa Wissef tapestry school or seeing some wonderful horses at the prize-winning Omar Sahkr Arabian stud farm, followed by dinner and a stroll through Cairo's Al Khalili Market in the evening. I was with the group going to the Arabian stud. It was apparently only fifteen or twenty minutes from our lunch stop. The coach driver had been given directions by the local guide, who had gone off with the tapestry party.

After half an hour of driving, I had the uncomfortable feeling that we were going off course. I asked the driver, who spoke hardly any English, if we were near our destination. "No, not yet, at least another half hour," he said. My heart sank to my knees and my stomach rose to my throat. I knew we were desperately off course by now and rang my Egyptian colleague. We discovered that the driver thought he was taking us to the Step Pyramid! The destination names were quite similar. Sahkr and Sakhira….. So I rang our stud hosts and explained our situation. No worries! He would send a driver to meet us and lead us home to him. Wonderful! We arranged a rendezvous at a petrol station and the car duly turned up. We followed him for some time and then, at a complicated junction, the driver vanished into the all-too-imminent sunset ahead, never to be seen again! What to do? I can't tell you how stressed I was. We were already an hour and half late for our visit. It would soon be dusk and how many horses could we see in the dark?

Somehow – thank God for mobile phones – we found our way to our destination. And what a destination! The most beautiful house set in picturesque grounds. We did manage to see a great show of wonderful Arab horses in the failing light. What a privilege! The Omar Sahkr Arabian stud had just been announced the best in the world only days previously!! Our hosts were charming and quite understanding and fed us with the most delicious tea and delicacies that I had ever tasted. Thank Heavens I had thought to buy them a gift from Fortnum and Mason! They knew this famous London grocery store well…. We found our way home with some difficulty through Cairo's dusty traffic and with just a little time before the evening outing. But, oh dear! No-one felt like eating a grand dinner after that tea!

The other party hadn't returned yet. In fact, they were completely held up in huge Cairo traffic jams. Lynne learned a few lessons about optimistic timing and how to accept some justified criticism for under-estimation of the length of an Egyptian hour.

More on the brick kilns around Cairo

There are two Brooke mobile teams which focus entirely on the brick kilns in the Helwan area, of which there are 174. There are no alternative veterinary services and no experienced farriers. I have an abiding memory of Dr Salah, handsome and elegant in his spotless white coat and grey-streaked hair, spraying Purple Gentian on countless wounds and sores as he singlehandedly moved about the donkeys in the brick kilns. Frankly, between you, me and the gatepost, though I thought he was doing his very best at the time, the job appeared bottomless. When I visited the brick kilns during this 2009 visit, again, I still thought the job was bottomless but that we had made such a difference. There was hope and light at the end of the tunnel. Yes, there were hundreds more brick kilns at which we hadn't even shown our face, but for most of those lucky ones which *had* seen a Brooke face, they were on a different planet.

Donkeys in the good brick kiln, Helwan

We visited two at each end of the spectrum in Helwan with Dr Amir as our guide. Both had been receiving Brooke visits for five years, yet they couldn't have been more different.

Our little group was greeted at the first brick kiln by its owner and his stableman who both gave us a very warm welcome. These two, the owner and the stableman, are crucial in determining the quality of life for the animals and the level of acceptance of the Brooke working on their territory. Sometimes one is willing and other isn't. Or worse, neither is co-operative. This can be a major problem. However, our hosts were proud to show us around their factory. It was clean and tidy.

Motorised trolleys loaded with wet bricks: brick-making machinery in background

Whomsoever we saw was reasonably clean and tidy. The animals were in good condition and their quarters were also clean and tidy.

They had plenty of shade and water and had good rest periods.

Tack was hanging up away from the ground in the stable. The amazing Heath-Robinson machinery which actually manufactured the bricks was fascinating to watch and all was in good order, with bricks neatly stacked and motorized vehicles rather than donkeys to transport the super-heavy wet bricks to the kiln. There was an air of purpose about the place. We left feeling very satisfied and optimistic.

We were then taken to the next kiln. There was no-one to meet us. The owner and the stable manager had kept away out of sight, though they had known of our visit. We wandered about. The place had a disconsolate air and the animals equally so. Many of them were not in good condition. It all looked so bleak. We went to the stable. It was filthy. The straw covering the floor had not been changed for eons. The workers were pretty unkempt themselves. The vet said, in a hopeless way, that he had not managed to strike up a relationship at all with the owner or the stableman. As was evident, these were the two key people of the kiln, the ones who set the discipline and standards. Good leadership is everything.

As is my wont, I started to explain to those men and youths in the stable where we came from, who we were. I pulled no punches and the vet translated everything. I said that the visitors here were not very rich (has to be said each time though everything is relative) but they had enough left over to be able to send some to help Brooke help you look after your animals and have an easier working life all round. Frankly, we were disappointed with what we saw here. But we knew how difficult it was doing this sort of work and that it was difficult for you to know where to start to make things better. Perhaps if you concentrated on only one thing which the Brooke asked you to do, you might find it easier. Just one thing for one month at a time. Then the task would not seem so enormous. We said our goodbyes and as we turned round to wave from the minibus, we noticed that they were already removing the old dirty straw from the stable. Even Dr Amir brightened up. So, who knows.... In fact, our stalwart vet was feeling a bit overwhelmed with the number of kilns yet to visit. So he got a dose of the same medicine! (And I must try to remember to take my own advice occasionally!)

One surprising fact I learned from Dr Amir: Brooke vets are being trained in Montessori methods of education. Most of the animal users in the brick kilns are children aged from seven upwards, so working with such youngsters takes special skills. The Brooke has been co-operating with an NGO called Spirit of Youth and together they have worked out a syllabus to educate the children working with animals through the three approaches of emotion, skill and knowledge.

The 75th Anniversary Special Presentation

It was the last day, the culmination of our tour. A special lunch party had been arranged to celebrate the 75th anniversary with Egyptian staff and trustees as well as representative staff from India and Pakistan. This was to be followed by an early evening reception at the British Embassy. All this and people had to be back in their rooms to pack and be ready for an early start the following morning! I had been quite involved in the planning of this Last Lunch, if not the Last Supper (might have made a few changes to that, given half the chance…). Endless chats to Egyptian staff and even trustees, hints and suggestions without wishing to appear to dominate the plans.

Some months previously, our Chief Executive, Petra Ingram, and I had discussed what would be an appropriate way to have a permanent reminder of this auspicious celebration. We decided that a picture presented to the Egyptian trustees would be perfect and I just knew the perfect person to execute it. One of our dedicated supporters had already helped us in this regard on previous occasions. Although he was 98, he was still painting and I knew would do the right thing. We would have a collage of Brooke scenes, with Mrs Brooke in the centre and a quote. I discussed it with the artist and sent him some photos to work from.

Unfortunately, by then he was rather hard of hearing (and, sadly, has since passed away). I would go into a small phone booth in the office where people could have confidential conversations and yell my head off, to the great amusement of the rest of the office, who could hear despite the windows. It was pretty hopeless, though. However, he said he had understood and would send me a draft of what he intended. This came through and it was marvellous. Exactly as I had envisaged it. Just one small point – Mrs Brooke was spelt with an "e" and the official year of our birth was 1934. I pointed this out over the phone. 1933 did you say? No, 1934. Oh, fine, 1935! No, no, I'll write to you to confirm everything…….. which I did, of course. The painting duly arrived in good time and was expertly packed for shipping. I therefore didn't want to disturb the fit-for-purpose wrapping. Our head of overseas operations, Dorcas Pratt, was willing to take the painting in her suitcase, which I thought was amazingly generous and stalwart of her.

Back to the party - after a delicious lunch, there were the speeches, all of which were very inspiring and moving. And the great moment was about to happen: the presentation of the painting. As we were moving toward the moment, Dorcas and Petra frantically gestured towards me from stage left. I hurried over, disturbed by their expressions. They told me with glum faces that, when they had unpacked the picture, to their horror they had discovered some errors in the detail. Everything is in the detail. But not everything was right in the detail. Despite my best endeavours, Mrs Brooke was still minus her "e", the year was still in question and our dear painter had thoughtfully added the flags of all our nations with their names above. But we didn't work in Jordon, we worked in Jordan. We didn't work in Israel, we worked in Palestine. Oh dear! I felt that bad. Why hadn't I opened up the wrapping? Why hadn't I double-checked that he had got it right. Why, why, why? What to do? Honesty is always the best policy. We decided to tell it as it was: present the painting, apologise that there were some minor adjustments that would then have to be made and that it would be re-presented afterwards. And that is exactly what happened. Everyone extolled the beautiful rendering of the painting and generously understood when it was explained that our wonderful artist – which he most certainly was – had misheard and misread some of the detail due to his venerable age.

The next hurdle was how to execute the changes. We couldn't tell the artist. He would be mortified. On our return I asked a dear friend who was both a water-colourist and calligrapher for her advice. She offered to come and look at the painting. She had brought her box of tricks with her – paint, brushes, pens, sharp knife and magic stone. The paper was, fortunately, of sufficiently high quality that it allowed her to scrape off the offending areas, smooth the paper back with her magic stone and add an "e" here, change a letter there, re-colour a flag here and change a date there. How she did it, I know not, but you simply could never tell. Honour was restored, along with accuracy.

We still had the British Embassy reception to come. After the inaccurate judgement of travelling times over the past few days, I was determined that we would arrive in good time. We did, so much so that the coach had to circle round the city several times, like an aircraft waiting for its runway. We were miles too early! All the anticipated traffic had disappeared because Egypt was playing an international football match. This also meant that the embassy speeches were squeezed into half-time, since half the guests (the male half) were crowded round a giant television screen in an ante-room. However, the British Ambassador, His Excellency Dominic Asquith, spoke from his heart and personal experience; he and his wife and daughter had just had their first encounter with Brooke's work when they visited a brick kiln and the Cairo clinic that very afternoon. We also heard from Brooke's then Chairman of Trustees, Major General Peter Davies and Richard Searight who, as grandson of the founder and a staff member for twenty-one years, provided the historical perspective.

Those Memorable Tours! A Wider Perspective

The value of Brooke supporter tours to our work cannot be over-estimated. Such a tour witnesses a union of all the elements constituting the Brooke: the animals, their owners, the staff and the supporters; and all those elements are moving towards an equal footing, towards a harmonious balance.

I quote from my earlier report describing the conclusion of our tour in India in 2007:

"The supporters and the vets exchanged superlatives. One supporter said "Seeing your work and how passionate and compassionate you are, we are convinced we must continue to work hard for you." Dr Manilal, (then the Head Vet in India), replied that he had previously had no idea about supporters and, having now met some of them, he was inspired to work even harder and to make sure that every penny was well spent."

And some further feedback after the 2007 India tour:

"Delighted but not surprised. Physically, mentally, conversationally most supportive and never obtrusive. That is Brooke."

"And I had a picture of a tree, green-leaved and beautiful, the rising prosperity of India in its boughs, and with Brooke vets working at its roots, bringing the goodness of the earth upwards to the life of the tree. Pictorial but, I think, fact."

Add to that the rapport and connection between the animal owners and supporters, and the owners' wonder and gratitude that someone far away is concerned enough about their beasts and indeed about them and the harshness of their life, you have a recipe for a more united world. All the ingredients are there. And that which brings the whole to a satisfying, inspiring and enjoyable outcome is INTENTION, everyone's.

For me, therefore, the Brooke supporter tours were the "bees' knees".

Chapter Four

STANDING UP AND SPEAKING UP

Apart from the many memorable moments I have recounted in this book arising from my trips overseas, as I already pointed out, going overseas was in fact a very small part of my Brooke experience. A very large part of my role within the Brooke involved talking about what I witnessed on those trips and putting them into the context of our work in general to a variety of audiences. I have had a wonderful time touring the country and speaking about my favourite subject. And there have been some unforgettable Brooke moments.

I was a mere eighteen when I first attempted to speak before an audience. I had been sent by my new boss on a secretarial workshop. I was the youngest participant. The last item on our agenda was public speaking and we were divided into groups to discuss and then present our ideas for improving the boss/secretary relationship. It was a competition. I threw in the idea to our group that a weekend in Paris for the secretary (without her boss!) could make a huge difference to her morale, self-confidence and commitment to the job; our group really went for that one! The older women decided initiation by fire was a fitting end to the workshop and put me forward to present our case. We won!

I didn't have another opportunity to display this new-found skill until I had been in the Brooke's employ for at least year or so. A stable local to me was very keen on the Brooke and had asked us to provide a speaker. I volunteered though I had no idea what was really involved. What was really involved was trying to make yourself heard from the front of a large barn to the back, over the heads of at least 100 people, with no microphone and hardly any visual aids except a couple of posters and some photos. "Can't hear at the back," someone shouted. So I raised my voice to operatic level and just let rip. The point about public speaking is that if you remember that the audience invariably knows considerably less than you do about the subject, you can feel a bit more confident that everything will be fine. You will know if you make a mistake or omit some vital point, but they certainly won't.

Since that first time, I have spoken about the Brooke on countless occasions to audiences of five to 205. It became an important feature of my job in whatever capacity that happened to be. Townswomen's Guilds, The Women's Institute, local societies, University of the Third Age (I call it the Age of Enlightenment), schools, riding schools, Brooke fundraising groups – they all called upon us to fill their speaker's calendar. Not surprisingly, what I had to present wasn't always appreciated. They were used to hearing about a beautiful foreign holiday, or origami napkin folding. Once I got going with the visuals, some of the audience would not lift their eyes from their laps. Mind you, quite a few would be fast asleep! But there were those highly sensitive ones who knew they wouldn't be able to sleep at all after seeing some of the sights I would show them. I was always careful with the photos I selected but people are generally unprepared for the rigours of life outside their own comparatively comfortable world. Two women walked out of one of my talks. They complained afterwards to their "commanding officer" in the Institute's hierarchy that it wasn't suitable material or what they were expecting.

One of the most memorable times was speaking to an audience of professional charity fundraisers. I was the last to speak and came after The National Trust, The British Heart Foundation, Guide Dogs for the Blind and the big Cancer charities, to name but a few. Nevertheless, I knew that our little Brooke still had some ammunition for the big guns. Each of the previous speakers had given very complicated and sophisticated presentations using "PowerPoint" which, to the uninitiated out there, is a computer software package which acts like a slide show. All you have to do is press a few buttons and hope that the screen behind and you are agreeing on the subject in hand. I opted not to use any visual aids but just to stand up and speak. I had recently heard an inspirational talk about the power of the heart and it rang bells. "You might notice," said I, "that I don't have any PowerPoint behind me. That's because this is my power point." I thumped my own heart as I made the "point". Everyone laughed and clapped. I went on to say that all our donors are coming from their heart and therefore the only way to meet them, for them to understand us and vice versa, is to come from the same place. The talk went on as I gave examples of how the Brooke works. Some years later, when talking to a colleague in another charity, she told me that she has never forgotten that presentation. "You came from your heart," she said.

Speaking in public isn't always plain sailing. Particularly when you have put all your slides in the carousel the wrong way round! I did this, believe it or not, at an all-male lunch! I hadn't actually used slides before. Lunch was delicious. It was great to be the only woman there. I started with great confidence and panache. Oops! Sorry about that first slide. And the next one. Oh dear! It soon became obvious that this confident woman didn't have a clue about her equipment. I could hear some male sighs wafting around the room – you know the kind. I didn't really give a great impression of our half of the world's population on that occasion. But I did manage to giggle to myself about it on the way home. And I resolved to get the hang of a slide projector.

Speaking to children can be tricky. If they are older, they are quickly bored. If they are younger, they don't always understand. I was invited to speak at the assembly of a rather elite public school somewhere in Westminster. The audience ranged from seven year-olds to seventeen, with all the teachers added into the mix. How do you talk to such a wide age-range. And I only had ten minutes of assembly time. I decided, as I stood on the stage, to talk about charity. What is a charity? Why is it needed? How does it work? How does it make you feel when you are involved in charity? How does it help? Many of the younger children in that school would have no idea of the desperate poverty in other parts of Westminster, let alone the world. I then had the perfect context in which to place the rest of my talk about the Brooke. Afterwards, one of the teachers came up to thank me for speaking as I did. "That was a very good approach. Are you a teacher yourself?" No, more like a sergeant major.

The talk to the fashion show in Northamptonshire was a memorable occasion. It wasn't so much the talk itself. First of all, what should I wear at a fashion show?! On the list of "attributes" compiled in the office for my 60th birthday, someone had written "Big Heart Big Wardrobe"!!! It's true about the wardrobe. That's because I don't get rid of anything if I made it or like it. I decided to wear a dress I had made out of a beautiful Liberty Veruna Wool (I still have it – Liberty Veruna Wool is a collector's item now). I had a little black wool jacket from Marks (I still have it – it's been faithful, so I am) and a pair of little black suede boots with high heels. Perfect! It had been arranged for me to stay the night before with friends of Richard Searight. The daughter would meet me at the station. "How shall I recognise her?" "You can't miss her – she looks like she could throw a bale of hay over her shoulder at the drop of a hat." I arrived at the station and duly minced off the train in my little black boots, Brooke Newsletter in my hand to ease recognition. Richard was right – you couldn't miss her. Her pillar-like legs were squeezed into an old pair of jeans over which she wore an equally battered jacket. Her black hair was cropped very no-nonsense short. I caught sight of her first. So I was also able to catch the look as she took me in from top to black suede boot bottom. We shook hands and she led me to her car. I daintily parked myself on the front seat and tried to find a space on the floor where there wasn't any straw. Did the baler miss some? Conversation was just as cropped as her hair until I started asking a few questions. We got to choirs somehow. That was it! We then found we had common ground.

By the time we had arrived at the farm where she and her family lived, we were on much warmer territory. I had discovered that she had a horse and, at her invitation, said I would love to see it. I had, of course, forgotten about my black suede boots. After negotiating the Northamptonshire mire at the field gate, I did manage a few minutes with her lovely horse. "Oh, don't worry about the boots. It'll brush off..." She then led me to a door in the farmhouse, apologising that she was taking me through the kitchen. Kitchen? Yes, there was a sink and I did see some vaguely white appliances, but the smell of rotting vegetation was everywhere. "Sorry about the stink. It's for the pigs." We threaded our way past rows of dubious-looking buckets into a rather dark room, the walls of which were lined with shelves of books and crockery and mugs on hooks, and newspapers and a large wooden table in the centre. Her mother greeted me very warmly and asked me whether I would like some tea. "Now, where's that teapot? I know I have one somewhere….." She rummaged along a high shelf and found an old teapot. Then the mugs. Hmm…

I was very touched by the fresh flowers in my bedroom. But it was rather difficult to climb onto the bed. It had been raised a couple of feet by the use of the underneath space as storage for some complicated carpentry equipment and a variety of saws. However, supper later that evening was a wonderful affair; I don't remember the food but the company was to die for. Mother, father, brother, sister and I were all gathered round the table and the conversation between us all was one of the most erudite and interesting I have ever had the privilege to be part of. I think somewhat ruefully of the house as Cold Comfort Farm, but its occupants were warm, absolutely charming and delightful. The fashion show raised a lot of money next day and the talk went well. My boots have never looked the same, however……

One occasion which called for all my intellectual prowess and presentation skills was when I was asked to speak about legacies to all the visitors at one of our House of Lords tea-parties.

Not only would I be speaking to supporters at all levels of commitment, but also to Trustees and staff (including my manager and the Chief Executive, who would be taking careful note of my performance.) Speaking about legacies has never been a problem for me but it might well have been a problem for the audience, many of whom don't necessarily want to face up to their own mortality over a cup of tea and a pastry. One reason why I have found talking in general about the Brooke quite easy is that I can speak from my own experience. I have seen the work for myself. I know what the problems are and how we have been going about solving them, adapting to circumstances and changing our approaches as we learn better ways to do things. But I can't really speak from experience about leaving a legacy! I ain't dead yet! I have thought about it, though…. Here's a little something I wrote for my regular Brooke Newsletter article on legacies, just for fun:

ON MOVING ON

When I die, it'll be such fun –
All those jobs I've not begun
Will wait forever, still undone.
I'll sit on a cloud with my Rooibosch Tea;
I won't be wondering whom I'll see
Or whether they remember me.
My body resting in its grave
Will moulder. There's nothing to save.
No-one will notice how I behave.
I've been corked up for far too long.
I shall be singing a different song.
My bottle will shatter when God sounds the gong.
Alleluja!

However, I digress…. Back to that presentation. I could more easily speak from my experience of including a legacy in my own Will – what it meant to me both emotionally and financially. I have included the Brooke in my Will. After all, it would not have been ethical, in my view, to encourage people to do something I hadn't done myself. I pondered my approach to the House of Lords audience. When it comes to writing a Will, there are so many aspects to consider: the anticipated size of the estate, to start with; then there are all the family commitments; and how best to avoid those swingeing taxes. And then it came to me. True inspiration! Benjamin Franklin once said that the only certainties in life are death and taxes. But, from the Brooke perspective, we can add two more certainties which life holds for some - poverty and charity. I proposed that by leaving a legacy to the Brooke, our supporters would be facing up to all four certainties and argued something along the following lines: their gift would outlive them and their immortality thus would be ensured; their estate could be relieved of a huge tax burden; they would be helping to alleviate poverty; and they could enjoy, while still living, the feel-good factor of being charitable, of helping the world become a better place.

The presentation went down very well, so well, in fact, that I decided to use the speech as the basis for a mailing designed to encourage people to consider leaving a legacy to the Brooke. We had an amazing response from our supporters and used the letter twice more, with equally good results.

The last presentation which I gave about the Brooke was, perhaps, one of the most disconcerting. I was shortly to retire and I therefore brought along my successor, the lovely Verity, to experience the experience. I was supposed to be the "expert" but all I can say is, thank God Verity was there! She turned out to be the expert required on the day. We arrived in good time at the venue, a beautiful church somewhere in London. The good ladies had arranged a sandwich lunch for everyone, including the speakers. There were two speakers: a gentleman talking about olive oil and me. Before I go anywhere, I always check what equipment is on site, what I need to bring with me. I was advised that they had all the equipment I needed. Fantastic! Unfortunately, although that was true, they didn't have anyone around who knew how to use it. It was complicated, large-scale stuff suitable for a large church. It turned out that the good ladies didn't even know where the church light switches were! We scrabbled around for some considerable time, until one good lady said she had something in her bag that might work it all. If only she had thought of that at the beginning! Verity put everything together. It was all beyond me!

By this time, I was feeling quite stressed and there were no sandwiches left. I'd lost my appetite anyway. The olive oil talk was interesting but long, and then everyone was invited to taste and buy. Of course, one talk is enough for anyone, especially after lunch and then having to make decisions about olive oil. By the time it was my turn to speak, most of the audience had vanished! I was left talking to a select five or six people, when there had been about twenty or so at the beginning. We gathered the chairs round and made it look as intimate as was possible in a cathedral-sized church.

Although Verity, after many false moves, managed to connect my computer to their screen, her success was debatable: one could hardly see anything because of those lights that no-one knew how to control. To add insult to injury, some of the good ladies were still busy in the kitchen, noisily chattering and clattering, while I was trying to get everyone's attention at the start of my talk. But, when two or three are gathered in Brooke's name, the magic works. The lights finally went off and I, with a sigh, finally got into my stride. All one can do afterwards is laugh and then collapse over a cuppa.

Heaven help Verity when her turn really comes.

Slow and painful
A donkey's life through all seasons
Engine of the poor

POSTSCRIPT

A few years ago, I was diagnosed with incurable multiple myeloma (cancer of the bone marrow). However, I was in the fortunate position to be able to start a truly holistic healing regime, rather than have to resort to mainstream medical intervention. I still continue my healing journey. You will be pleased to know that I am "stable"! But it is hard work! One day, I asked my Guardian Angel why he didn't just heal me. "I'm sure you can do it just like that! It's all so relentless, doing this every day." "Life is relentless", came back the reply. "Your every cell is relentlessly keeping you alive every day, doing its very best to heal you and maintain your body. The least you can do is give it your support, and honour and respect your own body for what it is doing relentlessly every day for you." I was suitably subdued and dutifully went away to take the rows of supplements, turn on my violet ray machine, say my affirmations and juice my veg!

Thinking about this, as I have been writing this little book, I realise that this is a great analogy for the Brooke Hospital for Animals. The lives of the animals are relentlessly hard, as they are for the families which own them. The work of the Brooke therefore has to be equally relentless, every day, healing and maintaining the body of the working equine population of the world. The very least we can do is to give our support, and to honour and respect the Brooke for what it is trying to do, relentlessly, holistically, every day, for the world.

Made in the USA
Charleston, SC
28 October 2015